Best of luck finding your best team ever!

JM

JOHN W. MITCHELL

PRAISE FOR DR. JOHN MITCHELL AND
FIRE YOUR HIRING HABITS

"In *Fire Your Hiring Habits*, Dr. John Mitchell brings his global perspective and extensive corporate and academic experience to bare. He takes a uniquely realistic and common-sense approach to embracing and understanding workforce development. I recommend this book to anyone who manages people in the post-COVID-19 world."

—TOM EDMAN
President and CEO, TTM Technologies Inc.

"This is the book I wish I had while commanding a Carrier Strike Group for the US Navy. For leaders in any mission-driven organization, John Mitchell's *Fire Your Hiring Habits* is not merely a must-read book, it's a must-do plan of action to find and keep the most talented individuals. His insights are just as relevant to the military and governmental organizations as they are to the private sector. Apply these concepts before your competition does!"

—KEVIN SWEENEY
Rear admiral, USN (Ret.) and chief of staff for the 26th US Secretary of Defense, General Jim Mattis, USMC (Ret.)

"Leading a team in turbulent times is difficult and *Fire Your Hiring Habits* is a refreshingly easy guide on how to do it well. This is a must-read for any manager. It's a deeply human-centered book, great food for thought in the time of multiple crises. John encourages leaders to see the situation as a Great Reprioritization rather than a Great Resignation. As CEO of the fastest growing European electronics company, I am deeply convinced that our focus should shift from technology, machines, and factory buildings to the human beings creating the value every day."

—RAINER KOPPITZ
CEO and cofounder, KATEK SE

"In *Fire Your Hiring Habits*, Dr. John W. Mitchell offers leaders a tellingly holistic guide to overcoming key components of the workforce development challenges we face today. His (for some maybe uncomfortable) spot-on analysis spells out what we all experience in small and large companies all over the globe, showing a path to a new post-pandemic work environment. Galvanizing, essential, visionary—must-read."

—CARSTEN SALEWSKI
Chief sales officer and member of the executive board, Viscom AG

"Finding the right talent has never been more vital—or more challenging—and Dr. Mitchell delivers thoughtful guidance and practical principles that will help any leader hire for optimal learning, improved collaboration, and better results."

—JOHNNY C. TAYLOR JR., SHRM-SCP

President and CEO, Society for Human Resource Management, and author of the national bestseller Reset: A Leader's Guide to Work in an Age of Upheaval

"*Fire Your Hiring Habits* is a book that bridges the gap between theory and practice. Dr. John W. Mitchell presents a methodical framework for addressing how you can understand and motivate your colleagues. Dr. Mitchell's emphasis on values and how they build culture and loyalty is a trait every manager should have. This book will help you to analyze, understand, and improve your managerial skills and increase your organization's likelihood of success."

—DIDRIK BECH

CEO, Elmatica

"Adapting to our new normal postpandemic poses a challenge for today's business leaders. Guidance from Dr. John W. Mitchell arrives at a perfect time to ease you through this transition period and get you on the right path to lead your team to new heights. This is a must-read."

—ELKE ECKSTEIN

CEO, Enics

FIRE YOUR HIRING HABITS

DR. JOHN W. MITCHELL

FIRE YOUR HIRING HABITS

BUILDING AN ENVIRONMENT THAT ATTRACTS TOP TALENT IN TODAY'S WORKFORCE

Forbes | Books

Published by Forbes Books, Charleston, South Carolina.
Member of Advantage Media.

Forbes Books is a registered trademark, and the Forbes Books colophon is a trademark of Forbes Media, LLC.

Printed in the United States of America.

10 9 8 7 6 5 4 3 2 1

ISBN: 978-1-955884-98-3 (Hardcover)
ISBN: 978-1-95588-499-0 (eBook)

LCCN: 2022921647

Book design by Analisa Smith.

This custom publication is intended to provide accurate information and the opinions of the author in regard to the subject matter covered. It is sold with the understanding that the publisher, Forbes Books, is not engaged in rendering legal, financial, or professional services of any kind. If legal advice or other expert assistance is required, the reader is advised to seek the services of a competent professional.

Since 1917, Forbes has remained steadfast in its mission to serve as the defining voice of entrepreneurial capitalism. Forbes Books, launched in 2016 through a partnership with Advantage Media, furthers that aim by helping business and thought leaders bring their stories, passion, and knowledge to the forefront in custom books. Opinions expressed by Forbes Books authors are their own. To be considered for publication, please visit **books.Forbes.com**.

Dedicated to my sweetheart for all her support.
Through the years, now, and into eternity.

CONTENTS

There are supporting documents available
for download, including color versions of
the diagrams you'll see in this book on:

www.JohnWMitchell.com

Scan the QR code on page 231 for easy access.

INTRODUCTION

I recently heard of a large retailer whose entire computer system is at least twenty years outdated. IT, consultants, and coders provide patch after patch. But what was once efficient and worked well simply doesn't anymore. In fact, there's just too much to try to "fix" it—the time has come to change over their system entirely to one that now serves their modern needs.

That, to me, is very much like hiring—acquisition—and retention in the workplace today. How do we recruit and find the best talent, and how do we onboard, train, and keep those colleagues happy and productive? Systems and thinking that were part of human resources, management, and "the way things have always been done" no longer work. In fact, anyone in the C-suite or management has known this for years. But there was no cohesive or innovative way of examining the entirety of the problem. So "patches" were added. People used LinkedIn, Indeed, or various incarnations of employment platforms. The onboarding of new employees was often a mix and match of various training and "shadowing" on the job. But the world of hiring, retaining, and even firing employees who no longer were fits for your company had greatly changed.

We were heading for an employment implosion of sorts.

Then, in the time between *deciding* to write this book and the *actual* writing of this book, the world changed because of the COVID-19 pandemic that touched all corners of the globe. An entire workforce—on every level—reacted and adapted. Changes touched every aspect of life, from teachers suddenly needing to create virtual lessons to restaurants changing their entire models of operations. We masked indoors and out and temperature tested ourselves and our colleagues in the workforce; we altered our social distancing. Corporations moved many of their workforces to online environments. People worked remotely—some moving away from where their offices were located. Life was irrevocably altered, and we had to figure how to do this all with the inherent disruptions to schools and government services, transportation, and travel. In this new world, we felt the strain—especially in my own electronics industry—of supply chains impacted by lockdowns, shutdowns, and absent workers as well as new (and necessary) safety protocols, along with what were perceived as labor shortages.

> **Instead of complaining about challenges, we need to embrace these moments as junctures in time for real, positive change.**

These "patches" and cobbled-together methodologies in hiring practices suddenly were placed under a magnifying glass. Existing problems became crises. However, disruptive social change also offers opportunities. This book aims to spotlight those opportunities with innovative ways to change the current, mostly outdated methods of finding, hiring, and retaining your best employees. Instead of complaining about challenges, we need to embrace these moments as junctures in time for real, positive change.

And while challenging, it is a testament to the human spirit, ingenuity, and adaptive nature of the modern workforce that such rapid changes could even occur in the workplace—not just in the United States but worldwide. These seismic shifts in how we do things haven't stopped. They are bringing about still more transformations that are reverberating as you read this.

Those of us in the C-suite, management, and the corporate world felt the initial pain—some wringing their hands—as the "Great Resignation" began near the end of 2021 and still continues as I am writing this, even as markets feel the stresses of uncertain levels of recession. I have a different view of it, perhaps from my years innovating in terms of hiring, training, and retaining employees in the electronics industry as CEO of IPC International Inc. Perhaps this was not the Great Resignation but, as some now reframed it, the *Great Reprioritization.*

So how did I become interested in "firing old hiring habits"? I have a doctorate in education (and my lifelong focus has been andragogy, which is the teaching of adults), an MBA, and a degree in electrical engineering (you can't spell "geek" without a double *E*). But over time, I have become a sought-after speaker on education, the workforce, and technology—both in the United States and across the globe in such diverse places as India, Japan, China, and Europe. Part of what I've come to really care about are not only supply chain issues in my industry but also *people* issues, especially as they apply to education, development, and hiring and retention—solving the so-called *skills gap.*

IPC leads education and workforce efforts for the global electronics supply chain, certifying over one hundred thousand individuals each year, leveraging technology across workplace and learning systems solutions. Over the years, both at IPC and in previous positions, I have been a change agent as well as an astute observer and action-oriented leader when it comes to hiring and retention. Some examples include the following:

- Continued practice of implementing modern workforce systems to attract and retain talent. This included remote work transformation in a company that struggled to envision such a change (and this was years prior to the COVID-19 pandemic), recruiter-less executive hires, and a culture shift for two companies steeped in historical "That's how we do it" approaches without losing their "special sauces."

- Creating a brand-new "start-up" division within a larger company—and interviewing nearly two thousand people on the way to building a two-hundred-plus-person team over a six-year period.

- Negligible voluntary turnover of staff over the past twenty years and three companies. Working through the difficult circumstances of necessitated layoffs—twice.

- Years lived and running divisions of companies abroad, including Japan, which gives me a global perspective on issues of staffing and workplace change.

IPC has especially led me to implement my ideas. IPC is a global industry association dedicated to the competitive excellence and financial success of its three-thousand-plus member companies, which represent all facets of the electronics industry, including design, printed board manufacturing, advanced packaging, and electronics assembly and testing. As a member-driven organization and leading source for industry standards, training, industry intelligence, market research, and public policy advocacy, IPC supports programs to meet the needs of an estimated $2 trillion global electronics industry.

IPC is on the front lines—hearing from members all over the world about the universal issues facing employers struggling with hiring and retaining in this brave new world. In addition, we hear about hiring and training issues that are unique to various countries and industries.

The workforce is not the same as it was in the early 1900s. Nor in the 1950s and '60s. Nor in the 1980s or 1990s. Or at the turn of the new millennium. Just as the "Greatest Generation" answered a clarion call to unite to battle dark forces in Europe during WWII, each generation, in one way or another, reflects its age. After such a sobering, divisive time beginning in early 2020, and as world events *continue* to unfold in an uncertain fashion, employees and colleagues are taking a moment to reflect on what it is they want from their jobs—and their lives—both in the workplace and outside it. Their self-reflection

> **We need to take a cold, hard look at what was and what is—and find the promise in what *could be* if we adapt.**

and the answers they are formulating are changing the ways we need to recruit, hire, and retain our most valuable assets: the people who work with us. And we in the position to hire need self-reflection as well. We need to take a cold, hard look at what was and what is—and find the promise in what *could be* if we adapt.

Strengthening both acquisition and retention of staff, we need to not just create a workplace that attracts and supports our employees, but a key part of our actual purpose should also be helping them thrive and grow as human beings (Ted Lasso style). People who feel they are growing, learning (because we should all be lifelong learners), and *valued* stay.[1] But the reasons employees stay right now are far, far different from the reasons in decades past. The reasons people stay at jobs may vary from culture to culture, country to country, industry to industry, and obviously from individual to individual. However, I think it is safe to say that in many places across the globe, individuality is valued more than ever before. Today, in the new modern workforce, we see chance takers and visionaries who are ready to throw out some of the old ways of doing things (maybe *all* of them).

My background has taught me that even if we recognize that our people are seeking something "more" from their jobs than simply a place to punch a time clock, to see value and worth in what we do, there is more to this Great Reprioritization than a resetting of workplace values and hopping on a bunch of Zoom calls. As we face worldwide labor shortages—and the impacts they have on every level of the electronics industry, food production industry, housing industry, manufacturing industry, transportation industry, and others—it is time for a great reckoning in how we recruit, educate, train, develop, and retain our employees and colleagues and build the spirit and culture of the workplaces we create, whether virtually or in person.

But in this book, I posit that we don't have to be experiencing a labor shortage at all. According to the US Bureau of Labor Statistics, the United States will add eight million new workers to the workforce every five years.[2] For the year 2020, China was projected to have 47.5 million unemployed people.[3] For that same period, Europe was anticipating 40 million available workers.[4] The latest statistics and the pandemic's influence on them will not be fully known for a bit yet. However, we know we have people worldwide who are unemployed, underemployed, or employed part time. It is *connecting* to these and existing workers that will propel successful companies forward—and that can be done by implementing changes in how we hire.

I set out to write *Fire Your Hiring Habits* as a way to open and expand the discussion on how we hire the right people; how we create dynamic, supportive, and innovative workspaces and places and environments—whether virtual or in person; and how to grow those employees and, in turn, our corporations, customer bases, profits, and contributions to the world. That includes how to retrain and cross-train, how to find the right employees, and how to challenge the old recruiting models that no longer work. But at its heart, this book is human centered. We can embrace this modern workforce age and do all of those things—hiring, retaining, and even parting ways—better than we used to.

With forward-thinking ideas and innovation—and a *Great Reimagining* of how we support and grow our employees as people—we can confront the unique challenges of this twenty-first-century workforce. We've come a long way since humans first industrialized, since our great-grandparents and grandparents punched time clocks, since the world was made smaller by the technology that connects us all but made larger in terms of possibility and change. The time has come to match those exponential changes with complementary metamorphoses in how we do things and in how we support our greatest assets: the people who *choose* to work with us.

This book will cover topics essential to the modern workplace, such as the following:

- Defining the elements of acquisition and retention of employees—and how they overlap in many areas.

- Taking a brief look (in chapter two) at how we arrived at this moment in the development of the workforce.

- Determining who our current workers are across ages and cohorts—and what research tells us they are seeking.

- Discerning how the workplace has changed—and how that has changed our needs as employers (and how we can use these changes to our advantage).

- Deciding how to find the sometimes elusive workers of the modern age.

- Examining modern recruitment: In the era of LinkedIn, how have our hiring practices changed—or perhaps more appropriately, how *should* they have changed?

- Verifying what the most effective onboarding methods are.

- Finding out how upskilling impacts retention.

- Exploring why diversity is so important.

- Ascertaining how we address when we need to separate from an employee who may not be a fit.

- Learning how we make decisions on layoffs and large changes affecting our employees.

- Studying how we train (and retrain) new and existing employees.

- Investigating how we make employees feel valued.

- Determining what our company culture is—and how we can develop (and measure) it so our talent wants to stay.

- Exploring how to best train and educate our workforce.

- Finding a vision of the future (and the future is now)— when all the elements we cover in the book work to create the best possible recruitment and retention methods for our companies.

- Implementing an appendix in which we explore every aspect of the book—and how IPC is handling it as a case study we can refer to for real-life applications.

In every chapter, I will offer real and practical observations and insights to lead you and your team and workplace into this thoroughly transformed workforce landscape. We'll "fire" the old ways that no longer give us the results we need in favor of embracing the transformation possible right now—within our sights.

CHAPTER ONE

ACQUISITION AND RETENTION

Finding the Best and Keeping Them

How many times do I have to teach you: just because something works doesn't mean it can't be improved.
—SHURI, *BLACK PANTHER*

My background in andragogy—how to best educate and teach adults new skills—means that I like to be sure we all understand the terms we'll be using throughout the book and how the elements of acquisition and retention work together. (I have a word that I believe I invented to describe this desire: unmisinterpretable. "Interpretable" means that you *can* understand the message; "misinterpretable" means that you *can* misunderstand the message; "unmisinterpretable" means that it cannot be misunderstood. This is the goal of all communication: conveying clear meaning.) The pathway of finding employees who are a fit for your company, onboarding them, training them, and then ensuring they want to stay has many moving parts. But in the end, most parts can be separated into either the acquisition or retention of talent.

But (there's always a *but*) they are a bit like a Venn diagram (see figure 1.1). Certain aspects of enhancing retention spill over to impact acquisition. A good example is the option to work from home. Particularly in the way COVID-19 altered the ways in which we live, work, and play, this is now increasingly part of our work culture. In order to acquire the best talent, you need to show you are embracing some of the new ways of working in the twenty-first century. However, this is also a retention example—people increasingly are demanding more flexibility and lives free from daily commutes … or at least hybrid situations. You can't retain the best talent without it. The grass is always greener—and people will go searching for that nice, lush green lawn.

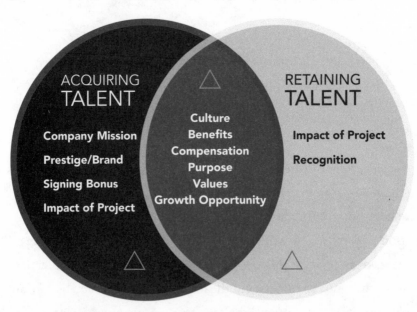

Figure 1.1: Venn diagram on the relationship between acquiring talent and retaining talent

As we discussed in the introduction, there has been a Great Resignation—or a Great Reprioritization. We might also call it the Great Reckoning. It is forcing us to look at every aspect of the modern workplace.

One issue related to acquisitions is the skills gap. There is not a shortage of people to hire—there's a shortage of people who actually have the skill sets you need to draw upon. In many cases, there isn't a **pipeline** that's been developed for you or by you over the years or throughout the industry, or even just in your local area. And without that pipeline, what do you do? It's time to get creative, and that's what this book is going to push you to do.

PIPELINE: A pipeline of people for an industry in its simplest form is a process in which a steady stream of individuals with the skills required is regularly generated. Many of these pipelines are developed in after-school or in-school programs in which skills and industry-recognized credentials are received.

This chapter will spell out the various areas of acquisition and retention as well as define some terms I'll be using throughout so that we're all on the same page—literally and figuratively. It will set the stage for the specifics of how to *Fire Your Hiring Habits* and transform the way you recruit and retain talent.

In chapter two, "A Glance Back, a Vision Forward," we'll look at how we got here (those who don't study history are doomed to repeat it). From the origins of industrialization to the surge in "knowledge workers," the past impacts our present.

In the area of acquisition, chapter three, "Modern Recruiting—Fire Your Old Recruiting Methods," will explore innovative ways of recruiting people to join your company. The old mindset relied on recruiters for executive searches as well as human resource departments. Both of those pathways found candidates and presented them to managers or C-suite executives for possible interviewing. With the technological advances of algorithms, that began to transform. Now, with artificial intelligence, social networking, and enticing new ways to attract and keep employees, there has been a massive sea change in how we recruit.

Today there are many innovative ideas for how to find people. There is not a shortage of people who could potentially join your company. It's that these people are seeking new ways of working and being. You offer certain benefits; your corporate culture offers the environment in which your employees and colleagues work. Potential employees offer their talents—but they are also seeking specific elements of work and benefits that are meaningful to them. This could be anything from green energy and a commitment to sustainability for one person, to maternity and paternity leave for someone else, to a position that is remote at least part of the time for another. The trick is making the connections with those that match your company's environment and available jobs. There are many new ways to find these matches. (Teaser for chapter three: I have never paid for a headhunter to find people—even at the very top levels of IPC.)

Chapter four, "Welcome Aboard: Modern Onboarding" isn't *quite* acquisition in the traditional definition of the word. The new person is already coming aboard or has been acquired. But they are

> **There is not a shortage of people who could potentially join your company. It's that these people are seeking new ways of working and being.**

not yet fully part of the company, and onboarding is not *why* they stay, but without being done well, it may be why they leave.

ONBOARDING: Onboarding includes the processes and mechanisms through which a new hire learns the skills, processes, knowledge, and behaviors to become an integral part of an organization.

Onboarding used to be called "organizational socialization." How is someone welcomed and trained, and how do they learn about your corporate culture? It also includes all the mundane but essential paperwork, benefits explanations, and so on in order to bring someone into your company.

Chapter five is called "Pathways and Upskilling: Growing Your Employees." This is where we start to focus on retention. It is nearly impossible to retain top talent if they do not see a pathway for growth or if upskilling is not offered.

PATHWAY: A pathway provides an employee with a trajectory and steps required for growth toward a career within a company.

Once an employee has determined their pathway, they have a vision and a direction toward which they are moving. While they are on that pathway, there will be other skills that may be needed to enhance that person's capabilities and talents. That is what we mean by upskilling. For example, if someone is on the career pathway to become a quality assurance (QA) technician, those pathway steps may include things like understanding the manufacturing process, recognizing defects, reworking products, etc. While on that career pathway or once achieving that objective, they will need to learn new technologies, materials, or processes to keep developing new and more advanced skills. In the QA case, that could include learning team leadership, new machine capabilities, new technology to reduce errors, or the latest version of software to lay out a new line more efficiently.

UPSKILLING: Upskilling is adding new capabilities relevant to changes in the industry or additional skills needed to enhance capabilities.

Chapter six, "Diversity and Inclusion: Making Room for Everyone," is a very important chapter on diversity and inclusion in the workplace. Diversity is always to a company's benefit. In short,

- diverse groups and teams come up with better and more innovative solutions,

- diverse organizations have a wider talent pool to draw from,

- diverse groups learn from each other, and

- retention goes up when people are accepted and don't have to hide parts of themselves in the workplace.

As an added bonus, I'll be providing a link to my website https://JohnWMitchell.com/book, where readers can take a quiz that will help you analyze how diverse your workplace is.

In addition, we will discuss *types* of diversity. Beyond gender, beyond race and religion, there are other areas of diversity in the workforce. We will be discussing diverse ages and each cohort's attributes, expectations, and view of work itself. Knowing what various diverse groups are frequently seeking helps you plan retention strategies—and recruitment strategies (there's that overlapping Venn diagram again).

"What's Your Company Culture? Attracting and Retaining Talent by the Culture You Cultivate" is the focus of chapter seven—and it's a very expansive topic. In terms of retention, it is essential that your corporate culture reflect your values and mission. People don't stay solely (or at all) for a paycheck. While obviously people must be paid fairly, the culture is what invites them to stay—they feel valued and part of something they are proud of. A negative culture for most people is not sustainable—no matter what they are being paid.

CULTURE: The culture of an organization is much more expansive than some think. Diversity of gender or ethnicity is vitally important, but it is more than that. Culture should be respectful of differences—whatever those may be: age, experience, geography, language, physical attributes, etc. The things that make us different are also those things that can help enrich our offerings as teams.

Changing a corporate culture is a difficult task, but it is possible. Doing so often requires very focused changes and clear communication with actions that support those messages. If we say we have a culture in which all people show respect to each other, and a disrespectful person is allowed to continue to act contrary to this edict—then that culture will not flourish. Another way to change a culture is to model it in a smaller group and then expand those attributes outward by showing the success of that test case.

Culture includes things like the following:

- Core values and commitments—the company mission

- Fairness

- A belief that the company is trustworthy

- Communication from the top down—and from all levels up

- Leadership

- Appreciation

- Camaraderie and community

- Diversity

- Transparency

And there is much more. In addition, in this chapter we will discuss separation—why it's important to let go those who don't embrace your values or who alienate their peers, creative a negative or hostile workspace, etc. We'll also examine how to separate legally and compassionately as well as examine the ethics of layoffs.

Next, in chapter eight, "Getting Help: Companies Are Not in the Education Business," we address pipeline issues and training, retraining, and educating people for open positions. However, there's one big problem: most corporations are not in the education business. This is where some strategic partnerships with schools—as well as innovative programs that can cross-train people ready for career shifts or position shifts without requiring years of expensive education—are essential. Like every partnership, you must choose wisely, discerning what you can handle internally, externally, or in a hybrid fashion. Fortunately, you don't have to do this alone—in addition to this book and my website, there are other excellent sources for workplace education.

Finally, in chapter nine, "The Future Is Now: A Vision of the Modern Workplace," we'll look to the future. I don't profess to be Doctor Strange in *Avengers: Infinity War,* able to see over fourteen million possible futures. We'll stick to a handful. If you followed most of the advice in the book, what would that workplace of the future look like? What sort of acquisition and retention methods will be in place? After chapter nine, our appendix will look at IPC's own approach to exploring all of the issues in the book in detail in our own endeavors.

🔑 KEY CONCEPTS

- There is a skills gap; the components of the solution fall into two categories: acquisition and retention.

- Acquisition has several aspects, which we will center on in chapters three and four: recruiting and onboarding.

- Retention is about meeting the modern needs of today's workforce: pathways, upskills, culture, purpose, growth, and the ability to make a difference. Diversity and inclusion, essential to the modern workforce, are also discussed. Chapters five through seven will address these subjects.

- Chapter eight will discuss where to get help in accomplishing these kinds of activities.

- Finally, we will bring it all together and provide you with some tools to better assess where your workplace stands in the new employment landscape as well as with a framework to assist you on your journey to better practices.

CHAPTER TWO

A GLANCE BACK, A VISION FORWARD

The Workforce Then and Now

You built a time machine ... out of a DeLorean?
—MARTY MCFLY, *BACK TO THE FUTURE*

We can't look at present and future ways of changing our hiring habits and work lives until we look backward first.

I'll preface this by saying that my company went remote years before the global pandemic triggered by COVID-19. I realized that my knowledge-based workers, the people in the office, did not have to be tied to a specific *place*. Their work was done in the ethers of the virtual or computer world. Their *minds* were their greatest assets to IPC. And those minds? They work anywhere.

Initially, because this was unusual or innovative for our organization at the time, there were questions. Some were simple logistics:

how to set up computers in home offices, how to file share and protect our data, how to "do" meetings. Would the company pay for office furniture? What about face time for career development? Other questions were deeper and more complex: Would people do their jobs as well without someone peering over their shoulders? Would their ability to take time to drop their kids off at school or their ability to make doctor or dentist appointments (or even walk the dog and attend to *life* in a flexible way) make them spend less time on their work? Would pursuing their private passions with more free time due to less commuting make them offer less to the office? Would they negatively take advantage of the freedoms this new system might offer? Or would this very flexibility enhance their lives in such a way that they were more productive, happier, better, more fulfilled workers?

The answer is obviously the latter. I am a firm believer that had our team taken negative advantage of the new changes we implemented, had our productivity significantly decreased, then I didn't have the right team to begin with.

A proven leader trusts his or her team. I trust mine. (And while I consider myself lucky in that regard, I know "luck" has little to do with it. But more on my methods later.)

I'm going to tell a simple story. It's simple because there probably is not a person reading this who has not heard something similar. But at its heart, it tells us a couple of important things about *now*.

I'm going to tell you about Jack. He was a director of a software development team at a company with thousands of global employees. When the pandemic hit, the company went virtual out of necessity. Jack and his team were no exception. However, the very nature of their jobs meant—in actuality—that not much changed in terms of the actual work so much as the workplace and the work *way*. How and where they were getting it all done changed.

Like most, Jack thought that the shutdown might go on for a few weeks. Maybe a quarter. But as time extended, so did the changes created by the pandemic. However, just as in all times of great flux, life did actually have to go on in some fashion. Employees and those in their lives had to figure out their new normal. Decisions needed to be made about what this "working from home" was going to look like—and where "home" was actually going to be. People fled major cities in droves as changes in how we as a society work, live, and play meant, for some, wanting spaces outside a commutable distance from a city or hub and into a location that might have been closer to family or offered at a significantly lower cost.

Jack—and his company—discovered that the change to virtual had no discernible difference in the productivity of his team. And in an informal sense, just looking at himself and his large team, for Jack (and many others) the switch was a positive in time and money saved by not commuting because of the flexibility and by a somewhat unmeasurable but still important personal quality of life. He and his team—and indeed most of the company—were energized, despite the occasional tech glitches we all experienced from time to time. Though no one would have wanted the circumstances that initiated the changes, there was no denying some positive work/life results.

Jack, meanwhile, made a decision to relocate. No longer tethered to a large (and costly) work campus and a lengthy commute, he changed states, and his team continued to thrive. As 2022 arrived and brought with it the tentative returns to *some* places of employment, many CEOs and decision makers and their teams were making choices and creating policies that now impacted a new kind of worker—a worker different from the one who entered the pandemic. For though the employees may have remained the same, their *lives* and what was *important to them* in an uncertain world, had changed.

Jack was advised by his boss that a return to the office full time was necessary. Jack clearly laid out his case that, in actuality, the quality of work and productivity stayed the same or improved while employee satisfaction also increased—not just for his team but also for Jack himself. It was net positive. He discussed potentially keeping the current arrangements with flexibility depending on employees and periodic in-person team meetings or gatherings (things IPC does a few times a year). His boss listened but, upon verifying with the higher-ups, quickly denied Jack's petition. The decision—from on high—was that anyone who managed *people* needed to be in the office. And so did the people who reported to them.

The ending of this story is also not unique. Jack joined the Great Resignation. And was snatched up at a higher salary by a company that respected—and, in fact, *embraced*—these twenty-first-century changes, a forward-thinking company as it pertained to what work life is going to look like moving into the next decade and beyond.

According to a recent PricewaterhouseCoopers survey, 83 percent of employers and 71 percent of employees term working remotely during the pandemic a "success." Over half of executives say productivity increased during the pandemic with remote work, and employees self-identified as 34 percent more productive.[5]

THE WAY-*WAY*-BACK MACHINE

So if we all recognize that times have changed—and changed rapidly—how did we actually get here?

Going way, *way* back to the late 1800s, most life centered around family farms or villages with farming as their mainstays and then those small "industries" to support that life—like a mill to grind wheat or a blacksmith shop—with tradespeople and those who worked within that system. If you ask me, a lover of fantasy fiction, what I think of when I consider the very first apprenticeship system, I would probably think of blacksmithing, which had some of the first on-the-job training. Blacksmiths had a skill. That skill was often passed down patriarchal lines from a blacksmith who came before. Only after time spent heating, hitting, and shaping metal over and over, arms exhausted until the apprentice learned, for hours upon hours, years upon years—until the apprentice could demonstrate his skills and capabilities—would the apprentice "graduate" … he, in turn, to repeat the process.

Making our way to the twentieth century, we note that a tectonic shift occurred. Westernized workers moved to live and work in the cities. As with many societal shifts, those leading this change lived through difficult adjustments. Long hours and six-day workweeks were the norm. Child labor was common (and in some industries desirable). Unsafe conditions led to avoidable deaths and tragedies. A lack of diversity or fairness in hiring or promotions was the norm.

In China, the move toward cities and factories did not occur until the 1960s and later in the century.[6] In 1952, 83 percent of China's populace was still in rural farming.[7] According to an analysis of the Chinese labor market by the Institute for Research on Labor and Employment (IRLE):

A massive shift of employment from agriculture to manufacturing takes workers out of a sector characterized by declining marginal returns to labor inputs and into one in which learning by doing, spillover effects, and greater possibilities for technological transformation of the productive process enable long-term secular increases in labor productivity.[8]

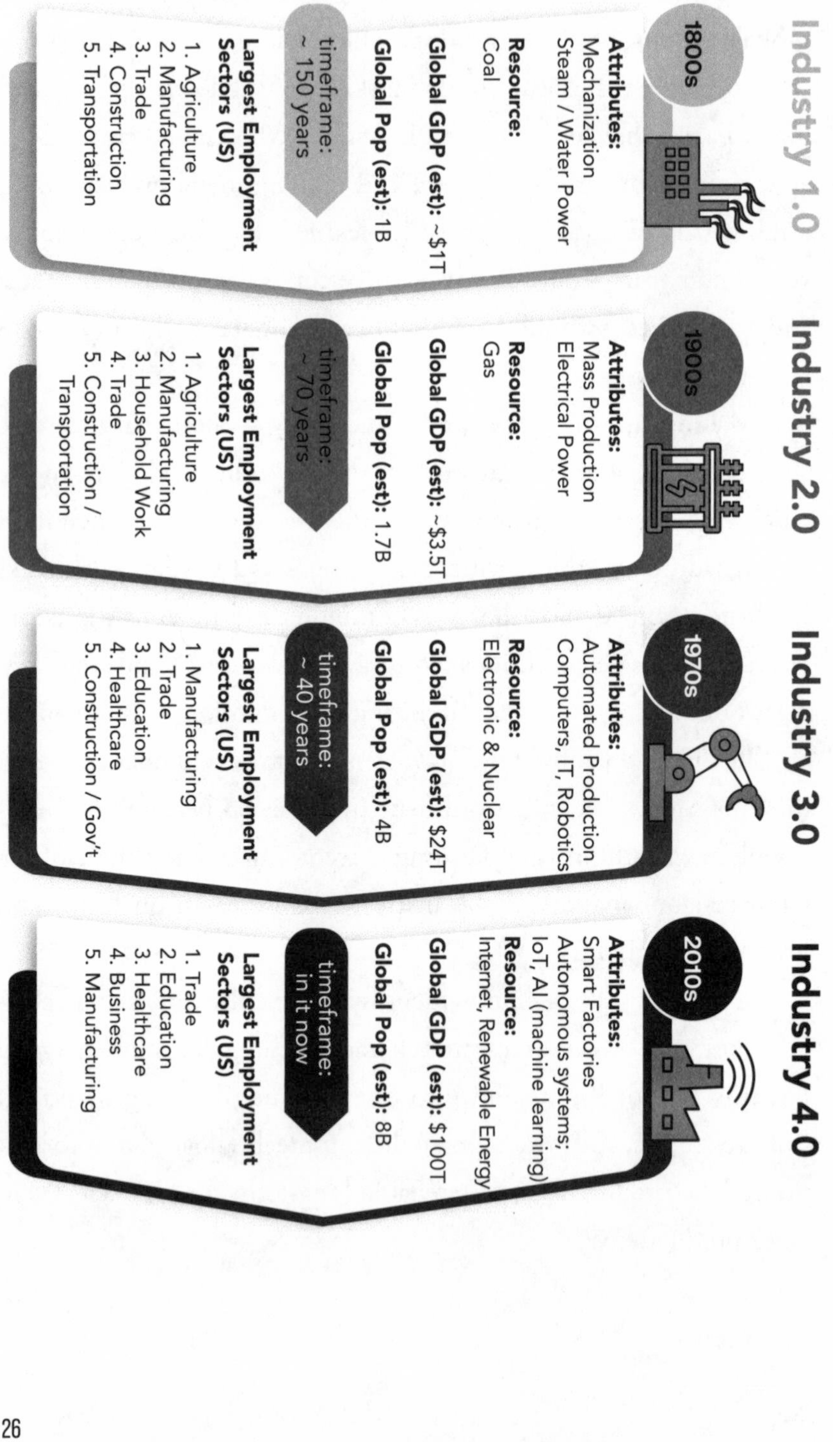

Industry 1.0

1800s

Attributes:
Mechanization
Steam / Water Power

Resource:
Coal

Global GDP (est): ~$1T

Global Pop (est): 1B

timeframe:
~ 150 years

Largest Employment Sectors (US)
1. Agriculture
2. Manufacturing
3. Trade
4. Construction
5. Transportation

Industry 2.0

1900s

Attributes:
Mass Production
Electrical Power

Resource:
Gas

Global GDP (est): ~$3.5T

Global Pop (est): 1.7B

timeframe:
~ 70 years

Largest Employment Sectors (US)
1. Agriculture
2. Manufacturing
3. Household Work
4. Trade
5. Construction / Transportation

Industry 3.0

1970s

Attributes:
Automated Production
Computers, IT, Robotics

Resource:
Electronic & Nuclear

Global GDP (est): $24T

Global Pop (est): 4B

timeframe:
~ 40 years

Largest Employment Sectors (US)
1. Manufacturing
2. Trade
3. Education
4. Healthcare
5. Construction / Gov't

Industry 4.0

2010s

Attributes:
Smart Factories
Autonomous systems;
IoT, AI (machine learning)

Resource:
Internet, Renewable Energy

Global GDP (est): $100T

Global Pop (est): 8B

timeframe:
in it now

Largest Employment Sectors (US)
1. Trade
2. Education
3. Healthcare
4. Business
5. Manufacturing

Figure 2.1: Industrial Revolutions and the changes within them

Over the course of the twentieth century, the composition of the labor force shifted away from farmers and primary producers, to "professional," technical, and service workers. At the turn of the twentieth century, about 38 percent of the labor force in the United States worked on farms. By the end of the century, that figure was less than 3 percent.[9] Except for the upper "elite," higher education was out of the realm of possibility. Most young people expected to go work in factories. But within fifty years, the number of factory workers had basically dropped by half. (You can see in figure 2.1 an illustration of the massive changes over time.)

Thus began the rise of the office worker or professional worker. We tend to think of this in terms of the 1950s "company men" (and they were, largely, white men), post–World War II, marching in suits and ties, briefcases in hand, to their offices, working nine to five (in better working conditions than most of the previous fifty years) at company jobs to work until retirement, collect gold watches, and play rounds of golf. The end. Women were held to supportive roles, like secretaries or typists. Diversity of race, religion, and gender and sexual identity was, for all intents and purposes, nonexistent.

In other cultures, variations of this value and mindset flourished. In Japan, for example, most executives stayed with companies their whole lives. In the last decades, that has begun to shift as well, as more than 35 percent of employees in 2020 fell into a "nonregular" category versus those in more "lifetime" positions, a significant increase (that has also ushered in more women to the workforce).[10]

What corporate America next had to figure out was how to embrace innovation and the rise of ideas. Instead of a hierarchical pyramid, a spirit of entrepreneurship led to an embracing of outside-the-box and creative thinking, especially in areas of tech and innovation. The best companies were learning to embrace the brilliance of diversity of all kinds—and the energy that generates—in a way that brought out the best of their employees and colleagues and, in turn, the companies they worked for.

> **We had shifted to a new work class: the knowledge worker.**

We had shifted to a new work class: the *knowledge worker.*

Peter Drucker is credited with creating the term *knowledge worker*—whom he considered our greatest economic asset. In 1992 he penned an essay for *The Harvard Business Review:*

> In a matter of decades, society altogether rearranges itself—its worldview, its basic values, its social and political structures, its arts, its key institutions. Fifty years later a new world exists. And the people born into that world cannot even imagine the world in which their grandparents lived and into which their own parents were born. Our age is such a period of transformation.[11]

In the way, *way* back machine, our parents and grandparents, and our ancestors before that, could never have pictured my writing this book on a computer—where I can access the libraries of the world and all the information I want at the tips of my fingers. Drucker was a visionary, but he could not have fully predicted the rapidity of this change due to global circumstances in the last couple of years. (Or maybe he could!)

SO WHAT'S THE PROBLEM?

Knowledge provides potential power. (You have to apply the knowledge for it to be truly powerful.) Therefore, isn't this age of unprecedented change and new knowledge a good thing?

Though this saying was originally intended as a nod to the sword of Damocles, for the modern generation, in the immortal words of Peter Parker's Uncle Ben (or, in the latest version, Aunt May): "With great power comes great responsibility."

The world has changed for the better in so many ways. As previously mentioned, child labor is no longer allowed in the United States and many other countries. Factories must be safe environments. Manufacturing is transforming daily thanks to artificial intelligence (AI) and the rise of smart machines. We are increasingly championing diversity in our work worlds. We carry our lives—our pictures, contacts of every human we know, our social media footprints, our e-reader books, our newspapers and magazines and movies and entertainment—and most of our work lives—in devices that fit in our back pockets. Heck, tech can now let us know with watches on our wrists whether our blood pressure is high, whether our hearts are beating irregularly, or whether our sleep the night before was restorative. As a triathlete, I can find practically any performance measure I want regarding my training with the touch of a button. A tiny button, on a tiny device. Or a swipe of a screen.

We also need not spend much time on the negatives—the cautions we must have with that responsibility. Most of us know we must keep children safe online, keep our *data* safe. There are privacy concerns and the proliferation of misinformation and even outright hatred.

We know about Moore's law, posited about the rate of technology increasing in the semiconductor industry. But this observation can be seen in digital areas too. In the words of Ferris Bueller, "Life moves pretty fast." But there's another piece to his saying: "If you don't stop and look around once in a while, you might miss it." Well, for many corporations and some in the C-suite, they haven't been looking around. These changes in the workforce have been happening since the way, way back.

But their thinking and innovation have had blind spots.

We've adapted to these technological advances. We saw life moving fast, and we grabbed onto the tail for the wild ride. Sometimes we've even gotten ahead of that comet. We've applauded these changes in our lives and our work. We were certainly all thrilled when Zoom, which was started by Cisco executive Eric Yuan in 2011, suddenly made our virtual work lives doable.[12] (Zoom struggled mightily in the beginning, by the way.) In my own industry, the transformations have been nothing short of the visions of science fiction decades ago.

But what hasn't kept pace with these changes is how we recruit, hire, train, retrain, develop, and keep our *people*. We still recruit pretty much as we did decades ago. If anything, for some workers it's even more frustrating, as résumés enter gaping black holes with hundreds upon hundreds of other résumés. Then it's sorted by algorithms, the ones that appeal to the algorithm head to someone in human resources, who then filters through them, and … well, you get the idea. I know someone who received a call from human resources to interview—for a position she had sent her résumé to eighteen months previously.

With the knowledge we have *about* our *workers*, we have the *power* to adapt and change and revolutionize the way we approach hiring, training, and retaining our people.

Worse, in a time of unprecedented changes, we remain laser focused on a set of "requirements," as far as degrees expected, credentials, experience, and many fancy letters after names. We look at that knowledge worker's polished résumé, and we want to check boxes. Yes, they have this; they have that. Oh, and they have this bright and shiny new degree. And that can be wonderful. But what about people who can deliver the *outcomes* with some specialized training without checking off most or any of those boxes? What about people who can actually *do* the work, but we place so many obstacles in the way requiring *years* of expensive and time-consuming advanced degrees that many of those people never make it into the positions we desperately need filled.

We also, as the business model changes, cannot keep up in terms of shifting labor. That's where my background in andragogy comes in. With the knowledge we have *about* our *workers,* we have the *power* to adapt and change and revolutionize the way we approach hiring, training, and retaining our people.

CAN WE BUILD A BETTER WIDGET? (THAT'S NOT THE QUESTION)

The fact is, we *can* build a better widget. With each successive generation, that "widget" has improved. Give bright people the tools to create—and they will.

So maybe we're asking the wrong question in this chaotic time. Maybe we should have been asking this question for years before this time (as I have tried to do at IPC).

How do we build a better workplace—one that supports the growth of the individual worker? And how can we change the barriers to entry and the way we train to get people onboard with the specific skills they need more rapidly?

I often ask this rhetorical question: Wouldn't you rather recruit a player who can get off the bench and immediately go on the field, ready to play their position from the moment they join the team or shortly thereafter, as opposed to a player you have to teach the fundamentals to first? Of course. And for whatever position, for whatever role that employee plays in the structure and process of whatever it is your company does—or produces—wouldn't it be wonderful if the people playing that position felt the following?

- They are prepared. They have been trained properly, and they have proven they are capable by *skills*, not just titles.

- They are challenged by their work.

- They feel *valued*, not just by the role they play in a process or company but for who they are as people.

- They are *appreciated*, Not just with hollow words but with real intent. Frequently.

- They are welcomed precisely *because* of what they bring in terms of their uniqueness—culture, race, gender identification, background, potential, creativity, and both soft and hard skills.

- They work in a culture that is one of pride, diversity, openness, and welcomeness.

- They like being part of the whole shared vision.

- They are supported as they grow in education and skills.

NO MATTER WHERE YOU GO, THERE YOU ARE

So now we know where labor and the workforce came from. But (with a nod to Buckaroo Banzai) *here we are.*

As we all know, it is impossible to put the genie back in the bottle (as much as Aladdin tried). Remote work is not going to go away.

People have glimpsed that there may very well be a better way to work in today's technologically advanced world.

Today's new staffers—and the values they hold—are not going to adopt the values of the past. Transforming the work landscape has had a cultural effect beyond what is going on in your workplace and facilities. There are new expectations on the parts of both workers and companies. Next, we're going to explore the modern workplace in detail—and the different types of employees and the values and types of jobs and motivations they seek. Ideally, we will use the tools and ideas presented in this book to unite the two—for us to *be* the workplace cultures today's employees seek and for employees to fill the needs of the workplace through innovations in hiring and retention.

KEY CONCEPTS

The modern workforce looks different from any other time in history.

- In the 1800s life centered around the family farm or small villages and towns.

- With the Industrial Revolution, life began to migrate toward the cities and factory jobs.

- As the twentieth century progressed, we saw the emergence of the "knowledge worker."

- By the 1950s white men (primarily) led the march into the office. These men tended to stay at their desk jobs or sales jobs for decades until retirement.

- Today's workers want to explore other ways of working. They also demand diversity, equity, and other changes to bring us into this century and beyond.

CHAPTER THREE

MODERN RECRUITING—FIRE YOUR OLD RECRUITING METHODS

New Ways to Find the People You Need

Rey: "You're offering me a job?"
Han Solo: "I'm considering it."
—STAR WARS: THE FORCE AWAKENS

The way job hunting is shown in the movies starts with someone having a cup of coffee at their kitchen table. They circle a help-wanted ad (Do they even have those anymore?) in a newspaper made of actual paper (increasingly rare). They call the number, aren't put on hold, are asked to come in for an interview immediately (apparently no one in HR has any appointments that day) and, without having *any* experience related to the job in question whatsoever—are passed along to the big boss. The protagonist convinces said big boss that they can do the job. There is no background check—for all the boss knows, they've just offered employment to a serial killer. However, usually it turns out that for reasons no one can discern, this person with no experience was just *meant* to have that job because, after some crazy mishaps, they save the fortunes of the entire company.

If only it were that easy.

Perceived labor shortages, the Great Resignation/Reprioritization, skills gaps, outdated recruiting methods, rapid changes in technology, and more conspire to make filling positions with the right people a challenge. But with innovation and a rethinking of the traditional ways of doing things, you can fire your old recruiting habits for new pipelines of employees.

THE SKILLS GAP

A **skills gap** exists in employment. There can be many reasons for that. For one, higher education is a behemoth. By the time colleges change degree programs to reflect shifts in career paths and job markets, the field ends up flooded with candidates. Or the desired skill set changes, or technology alters the landscape, or what was once a "hot" field isn't anymore. It takes years to correct things at the university level.

SKILLS GAP: A gap between the skills employers are seeking for a particular role and the common skill sets of those seeking employment at that corporation or in that area of work.

In fact, corporations and industries cannot expect and rely upon colleges to train their future workers (something we'll cover in chapter eight). So, very often, there is a mismatch. Or as many in engineering say, someone can graduate with an engineering degree, but they will lack the practical experience and rarely hit the ground running. The *potential* for a match is there because this new graduate might truly love engineering and be eager to learn. They are smart enough to graduate from a program, so they should be able to learn your processes—but it is anything but instantaneous.

Sometimes the skills gap exists for other reasons. Imagine an electronics factory in a medium-size city in a somewhat rural area. For years the processes have been largely the same, even as everyone ignores the *huge* elephant in the room. The processes need to be updated and upgraded to keep pace with technology. Robotics are introduced. People who used to work on the line are now being replaced—which sounds like *Invasion of the Body Snatchers*, but you get the idea. Not only that, but implementing robotics means that those pieces of equipment need to be set up, troubleshot, programmed, and repaired. The obvious solution is to retrain some of the people whose jobs are being phased out or no longer exist because of AI, robotics, or some other new technology. However, first, employees have to want to learn a whole new way of working. Some may decide now is the time for a career switch or geographical move. Some may be shut out of these new positions, with narrow focuses on having bachelor's degree or some level of schooling in order to apply.

That's a mistake.

You may be thinking, "Why's the guy with a doctorate in education saying a college degree isn't necessary?" What I'm actually trying to say is that we need to be judging potential employees by whether or not they can

> **It's time for managers and C-suite executives to embrace change in the "way we've always done things."**

do the job and what their capabilities are, not whether they check off a list of desired experience and degrees. There are many ways to gain the talents needed before, after, or without specific degrees.

I know that can sound pretty radical. But it's time for managers and C-suite executives to embrace change in the "way we've always done things."

Change or die.
—ALAN DEUTSCHMAN

DISRUPTIVE FORCES

Right now, and for some time, changes have been occurring rapidly in all areas of technology. These disruptive forces influence every aspect of our lives—including recruiting.

Let's start with **Industry 4.0,** the next Industrial Revolution, which brings together the assembly line with the Internet of Things (IoT). (Recall figure 2.1.)

FOURTH INDUSTRIAL REVOLUTION:

We are now in the fourth industrial revolution, also referred to as Industry 4.0. Characterized by increasing automation and the employment of smart machines and smart factories, informed data helps to produce goods more efficiently and productively across the value chain. Flexibility is improved so that manufacturers can better meet customer demands using mass customization— ultimately seeking to achieve efficiency with, in many cases, a lot size of one. By collecting more data from the factory floor and combining that with other enterprise operational data, a smart factory can achieve information transparency and better decisions.[13]

According to a recent McKinsey survey, more than two-thirds of industrial companies are making the digitization of the factories their top priorities. It is predicted that by 2025, 7.5 billion IoT devices will be in use.[14] Each and every day, we create 2.5 quintillion bytes of data.[15] *Every* day.

A related trend is Artificial Intelligence (AI)—machines that can evaluate their situations and make decisions autonomously. We have seen AI play out in science-fiction movies, and it didn't always go well for humanity. In the real world, AI is helping us make smarter decisions more quickly, and that's going to revolutionize the electronics industry and countless others in so many ways.

Another disruptive force is additive manufacturing, or 3-D printing. A few years ago, we were 3-D printing plastic prototypes. Today, we are "printing" complete cars and aircraft. In the future, doctors may be able to "print" replacement body parts that are perfect matches for the recipients without waiting for organ donors. With 3-D printing, we will be able to manufacture circuit boards and electronic systems with less waste and energy and greater agility and customization. It will open entirely new possibilities for the electronics industry.

In terms of recruiting and human resources, finding employees and hiring them, disruptive forces come at them from at least two directions. One is what I've just explored—we need employees with skill sets to fill positions being transformed for the rapid pace of technological advancements. On another side, the use of LinkedIn, online employment search engines, social media, algorithms, and other technologies in recruiting is upon us.

Additionally, the disruptive forces of the COVID-19 pandemic, a massive transformation in technology use to offer telecommuting and other options, as well as changes in what workers may be seeking in terms of what their job offers them and vice versa are changing how we recruit and attract the best people.

It's time to look at modern recruiting—how to fill positions from the factory to the boardroom.

DIY RECRUITING

If you want something done right, you have to do it yourself, as the adage goes. In fact, having a good team means you *don't* need to have that mindset. Your team should be more than capable of their tasks. But if you are a manager or in the C-suite, and you need someone for an integral role on your team, you need to be involved in finding those people in new and innovative ways. As a supervisor, you intimately know your team and the qualities that would create a "fit."

First, human resources recruiters and headhunters are disappearing. Those positions and the need for them have become scarce, killed off by LinkedIn (and Indeed, and other employment websites, some in niche professions). That's not a bad thing. But the odds of just the right résumé getting past the algorithms out of thousands, then narrowed down, and then landing the right person who fits your corporate culture (which we cover in chapter seven) is a long shot. It happens, but it's not an ideal formula for finding the best fit. It's a bit like the "Miracle on Ice" 1980 US Olympic hockey team beating the Russians. Among sports bettors (something I am not), the odds they were given were one thousand to one.

Instead, I will share that when looking for my executive team, I used zero recruiters for any of them. I found them via LinkedIn or other networking (personal or via sites) that connected me to them. I didn't pay a premium for any one of them. These are top-quality people, leading companies' executives, etc., who have joined my team through just a little bit of work on my part.

Especially in the field of technology, we in the C-suite and at all levels have often embraced dramatic changes. As CEO of IPC, I have a front-row seat for the advances in tech and

> **Without also embracing new methodologies and nontraditional sources for the human component and recruiting, we are stuck.**

electronics. It's an exciting, wild ride. But without also embracing new methodologies and nontraditional sources for the human component and recruiting, we are stuck.

If you want to be a successful manager or leader, you have to go after what you want—including the best candidates and people. I'm going to offer two real-life examples. In one case, one of the brightest designers and outside-the-box thinkers I've ever met ended up working with me. I preface this by saying he did not apply to the company I was with at the time. However, one of my directors had discovered him and his work, and we went after him. He ended up as the head of the user-interface side reporting to the director. So a piece of this new way of recruiting is spotting that special candidate—and going after them.

Now there's also another part of this same story. This creative man was not one to stay at any one job for years and years. Like many creative thinkers, he was someone who embraced change and challenges, new adventures. After a few years, he decided to part ways with us—a completely amicable situation. It was "time" for him and the kind of person he is. Now the *old* way of thinking is like Lucy in *Peanuts* running

FIRE YOUR HIRING HABITS

around in a panic: "He's leaving! He didn't stay for ten years!" But the new way of framing this—something I have believed in for a long time—is that for the time he was a part of our team, he *delivered*. He was the amazing asset that we had heard about. We were lucky to have him for the time we did—and I think he was happy working for us.

The key takeaway from that is people change positions and companies for reasons as varied as people themselves. If you accept this as part of the landscape of human resources, then you can plan for and take it into account.

FINDING THE RIGHT PERSON FOR YOUR TEAM WITHOUT THE USE OF RECRUITERS

My current methodology for filling spots on my team is the following:

- I stay consistently curious and open. When I see someone speak at a conference, for example, I pay attention to people who offer ideas and innovative thinking who might be matches for my company.

- When a position opens, I think about whom I've met and whose ideas I've admired, and I reach out via LinkedIn or their contact information.

- Of course, not every great person wants to leave where they are for a new company. That's OK. A no today might be a yes in the future.

- My approach is simply next-level networking. To any "no," my next question is, essentially, whether they

42

> know someone with similar skills and leadership.
>
> - I also peruse LinkedIn for people with the skill sets I am seeking and will pass those names along to HR with the instructions: "These are the *types* of candidates I am seeking."

Another example is one of my C-suite leaders, who was presenting at a conference—not yet working for us. One of my top people saw him speak—and because the mindset of finding the best people exists at IPC, he returned from the conference and said, "I think I have somebody you'll want talk to." My colleague was right—this person in question had great depth of knowledge and was exactly whom we needed. We shared why IPC would be a great fit for him. However, he was happy where he was. At some point, though, a while later, he decided he'd be a better match for us and would be happier on our team, and he came aboard. I believe we are both better for it!

FIRE YOUR OLD MINDSET

One aspect of recruiting candidates we need to address is your own mindset and some of the persistent myths that no longer hold true.

For example, very often, hiring managers might be leery of hiring an older person because they may think, *This person is going to retire in five years. I don't want to bring them aboard for the short term.* (Take it one step further—this person may have *already* retired!) This old/fixed mindset thinking misses out on great candidates (sometimes with a wealth of experience) because we still hold onto the idea—and this is largely true for different reasons whether you are in the United States, Europe, or

Asia—that we need lengthier commitments. Time to fire that mindset. Here are some facts from the US Bureau of Labor Statistics from 2020:[16]

- The median number of years that wage and salary workers had been with their current employer was 4.1 years in January 2020, a slight decline from 4.2 years in January 2018. (Note: In 1996 the median tenure for men in the US was 4.0 years, largely unchanged from 1983, so really, there was not much change over the decades.)[17]

- Demographic characteristics: In January 2020, median employee tenure (defined as the point at which half of all workers had more tenure and half had less tenure) for men was 4.3 years. For women, median tenure was 3.9 years in January 2020. Among men, 29 percent of wage and salary workers had 10 years or more of tenure with their current employer; for women, it was 27 percent.

- Median employee tenure was generally higher among older persons than younger ones. The median tenure of those aged 55 to 64 (9.9 years) was more than three times that of employees aged 25 to 34 years (2.8 years). More older cohorts than younger had 10 years or more of tenure. For example, among those aged 60 to 64, 54 percent had been employed for at least 10 years with their current employers in January 2020, compared with 10 percent of those aged 30 to 34. (Read that again if you still are wary of older hires.)

- Within the private sector, manufacturing employees had the highest tenure among major industries at 5.1 years in January 2020. In contrast, those in leisure and hospitality had the lowest median tenure (2.3 years). There is an age factor—

more younger people are in the hospitality industry. As of this writing, issues in the hospitality industry that were COVID-related will likely affect those statistics in the near future.

- Examining occupations, workers in management, professional, and related occupations had the highest median tenure (4.9 years) in January 2020. Within this group, employees with jobs in management occupations (5.8 years), legal occupations (5.8 years), architecture and engineering occupations (5.1 years), and educational, training, and library occupations (5.0 years) had the longest lengths of tenure. Once again those in service occupations, who are generally younger than persons employed in management, professional, and related occupations, had the lowest median tenure (2.9 years). Among employees working in service occupations, food service workers had the lowest median tenure at 1.9 years. And if you've ever seen how some people behaved toward service workers during the pandemic, you can imagine that figure will go down.

Now let's compare tenure in China to the United States. In the United States, we are used to the idea that a factory or industry sets up a large plant in a town or city. If the plant closes down, though some people will move for new jobs, most have settled near their jobs or were there to begin with. They are more likely to go seek new jobs in the same area. In the meantime, they are likely to remain in that factory for a long time, particularly if it is one that dominates a town. Management and executives are more likely to relocate as they move up the career ladder (how will this change in the era where more people are working online will remain to be seen). In China, one of the largest issues that's facing employers is turnover, typically at the production level. In the United States, 43 percent of manufacturing companies report production turnover of at least 20 percent.[18] Some companies are losing one-third of their workforces every year, and they must find people to replace them. That's tragic and difficult. (We will discuss this in the pipeline section.) However, in China, that figure can run at 40 percent or higher, depending on the industry.[19] There, production workers, too, are willing to move to where the *work* is, oftentimes to send money home to their families.

In India, there is a similar dynamic. Many Indian employees will go as far as Dubai to work in order to send money back to help support their families.

WHOM ARE YOU RECRUITING— AND WHAT DO THEY WANT?

For a very long time in the United States, Japan, South Korea, and elsewhere, in particular in those *Mad Men* days I referred to in chapter two, finding a position and staying there for an entire career was desirable. We know this is no longer the case. Employees have changed in countless ways. And so has the workplace.

In the diversity chapter and the culture chapter, we will discuss in detail how diversity of race, gender, religion, age, background, etc. adds value to your company. But there are also different generations, each of which has, in general, characteristics reflective of their age and time as well as different desires regarding their jobs.

You may have the same position—but your *messaging* when recruiting from these various cohorts will be different.

Figure 3.1 compares and contrasts boomers, Gen Xers, and millennials. What attracts a Gen Xer to your position will not be the same as a boomer (in most cases). As of 2020, 64 percent of millennials are managers with direct reports.[20]

Figure 3.1: Generational differences in employment styles and wants.[149]

While we will discuss flexibility and working from home in the chapter on culture, it bears pointing out that millennials statistically view their jobs as a *part* of their lives, whereas for older cohorts, the job may have been the main *focus* of their lives. For these millennials, flexibility for outside pursuits, for work-life balance, is important.[21]

While you cannot be all things to all people, and not every job is right for every person—even among those with the precise skill sets desired—in fact the same job *can* appeal to all three groups. What you need to do is offer messaging focusing on what is important to each group as you recruit them.

I'll bring up this point later in the culture chapter, but the primary reason someone comes to work for you when you recruit them will *not* be a paycheck. You need to value your people and compensate them fairly, but there is a blend of personal and professional values, expectations, and reasons less tangible than money explaining why someone is attracted to working for you.

In a large-scale survey from Glassdoor, results indicated that "money isn't a major driver of employee satisfaction.... For example, the culture and values of the organization explain about 21.6 percent of worker satisfaction in the lowest income group ... that rises to 23.4 percent for the highest incomes."[22]

THE PIPELINE

As our definition in chapter two pointed out, you need a "proactive" mindset when it comes to developing your talent pipeline. Here are some statistics that should motivate you and your company to develop your pipeline even further.

- By 2030, 2.1 million manufacturing jobs will sit unfilled because of skills gaps.[23]

- In a 2017 survey, 66 percent of electronics manufacturers said it was hard to fill production positions, and 64 percent said the same about finding engineers.[24]

- In ten years, manufacturers will hire for positions that don't even *exist* today, so we will need a nimble and robust workforce that can gain the skills they need to fill these positions.

- The talent gap is exacerbated by evolving demographics: millennials are less interested in manufacturing industry careers, and the majority of US adults don't encourage their children to enter the sector.[25]

We have to find new ways to ensure that we have the talent we need (see figure 3.2).

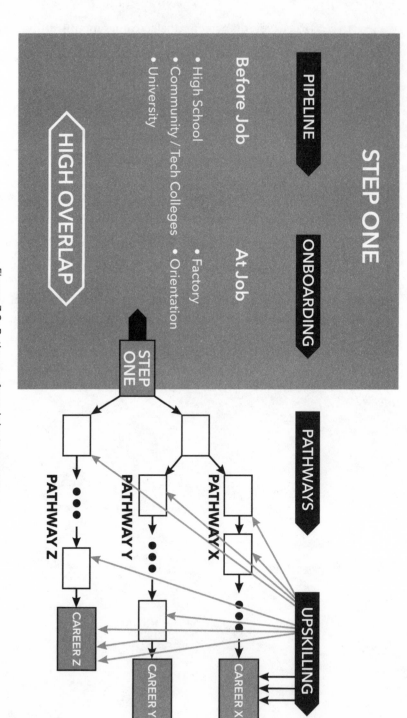

Figure 3.2: Pathways from jobs to careers

THE GAUNTLET

We *urgently* need to devise programs that can rapidly get candidates up to "good enough." From there, you continue to enhance their training over the years.

I will discuss this further in chapter four, but I was impressed with a program I refer to as "the Gauntlet." The idea was to take candidates from other fields or without specific experience to the electronics job that needed filling and retrain them *quickly* and *intensively* in a matter of weeks (or days) to be able to fill a slot on the assembly line.

> It's important to show employees a clear path to continue their careers with your company with further education and training.

Taking that idea a step further, I feel that it's important to show employees a clear path to continue their careers with your company with further education and training.

JOB FAIRS

In a book about innovation in your hiring habits, what's so innovative about a job fair?

It's *rethinking* the job fair. This is an actual example of a member company of IPC looking for people for their electronics factory. They set a specific day for the job fair, advertised it, blasted it on social, and offered incentive bonuses for employee referrals. They invited people in at eight o'clock in the morning, and they give them a tour of the factory—and all its positives. They talked about their company—and in the very important culture chapter, we discuss what corporations today need to have as far as their culture in order to attract the best candidates, whether they are production workers, middle managers, or C-suite executives. Remember, people choose jobs for more than drawing a paycheck. In addition, then and there, the company in this case showed their visitors the kinds of jobs that they were looking to fill. Then they interviewed the people who came to their job fair and made job offers all within three to four hours. They were done. And they had people starting the following Monday.

Why was this so successful? First, for someone out of work, the idea that they could be in training on Monday instead of in weeks of interviews and delays is a completely positive experience. Second, when people accept a job offer, it is because they can *see* themselves in that position. By the company holding this in-person tour, candidates could literally see where they would be working and what they would be doing in a tangible way. Third, hopefully your culture is a happy one (we'll discuss the Happy Marriott case in the culture chapter). Having the candidates go through this process, feel valued on the tour, and see potential coworkers content at their jobs added to a momentum of wanting to come aboard.

RECRUITING PEOPLE YOU KNOW

In *Hard Facts, Dangerous Half-Truths, and Total Nonsense: Profiting from Evidence-Based Management*, by authors Jeffrey Pfeffer and Robert I. Sutton, the authors discuss the dangerous half-truth that you shouldn't hire relatives or people you know because of nepotism. But it is a half-truth—on the one hand, that is definitely something to be cautious about. If you have ever worked in a situation in which a family-owned company has significant issues between family members, you know it can be a recipe for dysfunction.

But what's the other half?

When you're interviewing somebody, the total time, if you are lucky, might amount to three hours of exposure of that person to your team. I know that in one case where I worked, they were very thorough, and I had probably twelve hours of exposure when I was hired. While that can sound like a lot in terms of interviewing time, in reality, it's only twelve hours compared to perhaps years at a position. However, if I know somebody, if I've worked with them, if I have a family member or a friend, and I refer them, I have had years of experience with them. And I know whether they're a hard worker, whether they're loyal, whether they have integrity—all of those things that you can only guess at in an interview.

Two caveats. One, the person referring the candidate should be someone whose insights you trust. You don't want a situation in which their sister's wayward nephew who has never done a day's work in his life and can't get a job anywhere else is offered a spot that could go to someone more deserving.

In addition, you need to be willing to fire that person, just the same as any other employee, if they do not perform. We will discuss separation and letting people go, as well as layoffs, in the culture chapter.

SIGNING BONUSES

As I'm writing this, there are many jobs going unfilled, and there is a sense of scarcity of *people* (even if this is not actually true); signing bonuses are once again being used to recruit (something that we have not seen in several years). However, by the time this book is published, given the speed at which things are changing in a very volatile world, there's no telling.

Signing bonuses are typically 5 to 20 percent of an employee's yearly salary. Oftentimes, there are stipulations. For example, if an employee exits before a certain period of time, they may be required to pay back some portion of the signing bonus.

Signing bonuses can play a part in the recruiting process, particularly if your competition is offering them. However, I have an additional caveat. If one of your executives or managers comes in and asks for a bonus in order for them not to "walk" to another offer they have in hand, my standard advice is to let them go. That person has one foot out the door already.

INTERNSHIPS VERSUS SHADOWING VERSUS APPRENTICESHIPS

Internships are very effective because they offer on-the-job training. They are also wonderful ways to get around that "three hours" of interview time. You get to see firsthand this potential employee's work ethic, how they get along with the team, their energy and passion. Think of it as a three-to-six-month employment test, a recruiting tool.

Job shadowing is different (and we'll discuss this in the onboarding chapter next). The problem with shadowing is that you can assign a new employee to someone who is brilliant at their position but a lousy teacher. Teaching is not everyone's gift. In addition, a new employee may need many hours to assimilate into a specific position—and the person they are shadowing may not have the time to invest in them properly.

Apprenticeships are often confused with internships, especially in the United States. The key differentiators I've found are clearer in Europe. Those in apprenticeships usually spend more time there (over one year) and end up with some sort of credentials demonstrating the skills they have obtained. An internship is about gaining experience specific to the company where that individual has worked.[26]

THE RULE OF THREE

The Rule of Three is essential in the recruiting and hiring process. One interpretation of the Rule of Three is to insist that the final interviews be whittled to *three* candidates. The following points are based on the ideas of Ram Charon.[27] The advantages of this number include the following:[28]

- Maintaining an open mind. Rather than honing in on a singular candidate, you can broaden the process and compare and contrast to help zero in on specific traits and skills you see in one candidate over the other.

- Searching deeper. It is daunting to find even one "perfect" candidate to fill an executive position. Two seems lucky. Three? By using the Rule of Three, your search must cast a wide net and also dive deep.

- Who is the match? It is unlikely you will get three identical candidates unless they're clones. They may have similar career and educational backgrounds, similar experience, etc. However, they will not have the same personalities or the same philosophies, and they should be diverse and bring their own personal contributions to your team based on their uniqueness. Your corporate culture is essential to a positive and productive workplace. By using the Rule of Three, you will have a better opportunity to discern the best match.

My own Rule of Three is that in the interview process for managers and executives, there should be a narrowing down of three different candidates, interviewed three different times, by three different people, at three different venues. It is too easy in a singular interview to only get a "snapshot" of the candidate, how they present themselves at that one point in time. That is actually one of the reasons I am not a huge fan of personality tests such as the Dominance, Influence, Steadiness, and Conscientiousness (DiSC) test as part of the hiring process. First, people unconsciously or consciously try to give the "right" answers, not their truthful answers. It is also the test at that precise moment in time. We evolve, change, and act in different ways depending on situations.

New Recruiting
CHECKLIST

Different Places to Find Potential Talent

☐ Everyday encounters – restaurants, coffee houses, etc.

☐ Don't rely solely on headhunters or recruiters

☐ Simple online postings at places like LinkedIn / Indeed

☐ Targeting specific individuals

☐ Speakers at conferences or seminars (online or live)

☐ Internal staff desirous for new skills / opportunities

☐ LinkedIn search – examples of talent you're seeking

☐ Association events – networking directly or indirectly

☐ Companies or groups in different industries

☐ Recent retirees – could be part-time or contract

☐ Staff contacts (friends, acquaintances, relatives)

☐ Try before you buy – internships, shadowing, contract/project work

Things to Remember When Recruiting

☐ Supervisor direct involvement

☐ Know who you are speaking with – adjust accordingly

☐ Rule of Three: different people, places, times

☐ Highlight what *they* are looking for in your organization

Figure 3.3: New Recruiting Checklist

🔑 KEY CONCEPTS ─────────────────────────

Modern recruiting looks very different from any other time in history. Before we move ahead to Onboarding, let's recap:

- Modern recruiting has largely changed the landscape of finding people—and enticing them to come to your team.

- As Alan Deutschman said, "Change or die." Accept and embrace this brave new world.

- We have a skills gap that is impacting many industries—but especially electronics.

- Disruptive forces are changing every aspect of our lives, especially in technology.

- Human resources departments are disappearing. Recruiting firms are dying off.

- With the advent of LinkedIn, other employment apps, and technologies that help in recruiting, there are entirely new ways of finding people.

- Managers *must* be involved in finding talent.

- Always be on the lookout for talent—and then pursue candidates.

- The old model of staying at a job for decades is gone. People switch jobs with more frequency—accept it and reframe your thinking.

- Different cohorts want different things from their jobs and careers. Adjust your messaging accordingly to appeal to each.

- To compensate for the skills gap and to ensure you find the people you need, you must develop your own pipelines. These can include:

  - programs like the Gauntlet that train and bring people aboard quickly—and are based on learned skills and competencies, not specific requirements;

  - innovative job fairs;

  - people you know / referrals; and

  - the Rule of Three.

All right—you've found your people using new and innovative recruiting methods. Now it's time to bring them on board in the next chapter.

CHAPTER FOUR

WELCOME ABOARD

Modern Onboarding

Permission to come aboard?

—AQUAMAN

From *Transcendence* to *The Matrix* to *Altered Carbon*, Hollywood and the amazing geniuses working in AI imagine that one day we'll just transfer consciousness from one person to another with a microchip. For now, that's just in the movies.

If only information transfer were that easy.

However, in our present reality, we have to put steps in place to bring new hires aboard. As you recall from chapter two, onboarding comprises the process and mechanisms through which new hires learn the skills, processes, knowledge, and behaviors to become integral to your organization.

Think about a parent with three kids at three different schools, along with two dogs and one cat. The oldest dog can only walk a half a block. Each kid does one after-school activity—all different activities but at different times. Each kid has different friends, one child is allergic to wheat, and the youngest gets sick any time he's in the car for more than ten minutes. Suddenly, that parent has to make an unexpected work trip, so they enlist their childless brother to watch the kids in this emergency for two days. If the parent left an actual list of everything Uncle Buck has to remember and do and where to drive, etc., it would require, well, a thick book like the employee manuals some companies hand out. Information transfer is something we deal with in all aspects of our lives.

Onboarding an employee also requires information transfer. And no two companies do it the same way. But typically (at least in recent times) most companies have some sort of video. In large companies, these can be as professionally produced as a Hollywood film, explore the company's mission, include interviews with people throughout the organization, examine its global presence, and provide overall information. Some companies now use computer modules to view and answer short quizzes in between sections. Most companies offer a benefits overview that explains what the healthcare choices are, how many days off the new employee can take, which holidays the company offers, etc. For this kind of information, that's probably "good enough." This type of onboarding is often vernacularly called "orientation." There's an employee handbook. You can have references for the kind of information that is basic, without a lot of nuance or learning. If this information is transferred poorly by a person, there's a place somewhere that the new employee can go to get the information.

Poor Uncle Buck just has to deal with the kid getting sick in the back of the car.

ONBOARDING SKILLS

When onboarding real skills, though—the skills employees need to actually *do* their jobs—that's where we have problems across the entire spectrum of jobs, from the factory floor on up.

Right now in many companies, onboarding is a haphazard affair at best. Knowledge and skills transfers are a bit like throwing the proverbial spaghetti against the wall: some things stick.

And some do not.

Imagine the world's greatest mentor who could be assigned to you (as a new employee). You'd be in seventh heaven. They're patient. They have an organized way of explaining various tasks. They'll introduce you to coworkers to make your transition easier and make you feel more welcome. They'll network. They'll bring you into meetings. They'll show you what you're going to be doing. They'll help draw questions out of you. All of that good stuff—except I don't know actually know anyone who's had that experience.

I'm sure it's out there. Somewhere. Just like that microchip that's going to do knowledge transfer directly to your brain. It's a bit of a fiction.

I have my own personal experience with this. I was at a household-name multinational corporation. I was assigned to a very brilliant man. He was one of those go-to guys in the company. He knew so much that, in their minds, they had given me an exceptional person to learn from. Maybe three days into my job, he talked through various aspects of the job and company with me for maybe an hour.

He was very cordial and clearly knowledgeable, and at the end of that hour, he said, "If you have any other questions, ask me." I am sure in his mind, his mentor interaction with me was largely complete.

I maybe went to him once more. Why? This methodology has some obvious problems:

- People with that kind of knowledge and skills in the company are very busy. They already *have* another job. They're doing very valuable work. Thus, you are tying up your most valuable resources to do something that they're not trained to do.

- You don't know what you don't know. So you don't know what to ask. Some people enter companies in positions of strength in that they arrive with strong skill sets already—but others are starting from zero.

- Another common issue is that you learn "the right way" to do things in different ways, depending on who your team leader or trainer is. There is no consistency.

- As someone who loves learning, I know that not everyone is a natural-born teacher. I'm sure you can think back through various instructors, teachers, and mentors and recall the standout ones—as well as the ones whose lectures felt like watching the proverbial paint dry.

CONSISTENCY IS NOT THE HOBGOBLIN

Many people are mistaken about the old adage from Ralph Waldo Emerson. The phrase is not "Consistency is the hobgoblin of little minds" but "*Foolish* consistency is the hobgoblin of little minds." Consistency doesn't indicate a lack of vision or a rut. Consistency is your friend when it comes to onboarding.

First, if you can find a program that can give you the right set of skills that is industry specific—grab it. This can be a big plus, especially if it's offered at a low cost. Most companies (especially smaller ones) are cautious about where to spend. However, a $500 program that's going to make their employees more effective and faster and offer a consistent knowledge transfer is well worth it. Here's another old adage: don't be penny wise and pound foolish.

For example, in IPC's industry, a common issue concerns very bright engineers coming out of school without the practical knowledge they need. They know the formulas. They know "classroom" engineering, but most have never actually had practical experience. A program that can bring *every* engineer to the same skill level (not just the ones with great mentors) is well worth it.

To look at it another way, as opposed to someone you are paying $150 an hour (and who may or may not be a good trainer) using their time to teach a new employee, perhaps the $500 you spend on a program gets you forty hours of clear, well-produced instruction. Not only that, but the new hire can also refer back to that program again and again—versus hounding your "expensive" employee with follow-up questions (if they can even track them down to ask).

The brilliant mentor still has a purpose. But instead of using their expertise for generalized training, you can go to that person for the specific things that broad, industry-wide training can't offer you. And we actually have found this to be true at IPC. We developed training on electronics assembly for engineers. The idea is that an engineer can come in, and they are not going to know everything it takes to work on or with the factory floor. Instead, they can have this resource for a few hundred dollars, and now they've got thirty to forty hours of content that they can grab and retake and look at anytime they need to refer back—I've seen this work firsthand.

Well-designed programs are also done using many learning modalities. So it's not just "death by PowerPoint." When you're looking for onboarding programs, you want to get as far as you can with automated processes before you get to the specifics that are unique to just your company.

I hate the way people use slide presentations instead of thinking.
—STEVE JOBS

Another mistake that many companies make is that they think their company is unique in every single way. They "reinvent the wheel"—over and over. However, if they're lucky, they're 10 to 15 percent unique in their given industry. So why not buy the other 85 percent to 90 percent of onboarding so that you don't have to think about it anymore (or further tie up your precious internal talent)?

A good example is the brilliant CEO who goes out and mows his lawn instead of hiring the kid down the street to do it. Now if it's therapeutic for that CEO, they are getting other value from this task. But if this CEO is burning up two hours of their day on Saturday, when they could instead be doing something else (such as family time toward a work-life balance) or networking or doing much higher-value work, then paying fifty bucks to the neighborhood kid makes a lot more sense. Come to think of it, the CEO isn't that brilliant after all.

You need to ask yourself: What are the onboarding problems I am trying to solve? This can range from consistency to information overload to a more urgent current problem—onboarding remote workers.

When companies are seeking to have more effective onboarding to get their new employees off the proverbial benches and into playing time as soon as possible, they need to be looking for help. And when you're looking for help, what are the things you should be looking for first? One is that it needs to be *cost effective*. Too many get stuck when they hear "cost," but the operative word there is "effective."

You also need to determine the various levels of jobs you have. Typical categories that I use in my industry are as follows:

- Production

- Technicians

- Engineers

- Management

- Executives

Each level requires differing degrees of training and choosing to purchase a program for onboarding; this position should also reflect the level. Programs for production staff would be the least expensive. You can expect costs to increase by a factor of two to four per level.

Another aspect is certification. I believe we should be less concerned with very narrowly defined checklists of degrees for certain positions. Certifications are (depending on industry and position) more important. *Can you do the job?* Ideally for, say, production employees or technicians, you'd like to find new employees who are already up to speed and certified. However, if that is not the case, then providing training to get from uncertified to certified quickly is essential.

THE GAUNTLET

I often refer to a program I like to call "the Gauntlet." This refers to an onboarding process that very rapidly gets people on board. For example, we can take someone from the banking or food industry into a new job in the electronics industry working skillfully within a couple of days. Programs like these are transforming onboarding. I know of a program that, in 2009, took individuals with zero relevant experience and got them from the bench to the playing field in nine weeks. I call it the Gauntlet because in that particular program, at the end of each week of instruction, if you didn't pass—you were out. Out of the program. Hence the Gauntlet.

There are Gauntlet-like programs at community colleges. Sometimes a company will partner with the college for a short-term course teaching a certification.

In 2022, the nine weeks from the reference above is accomplished in nine to eighteen *hours*.

How has this process condensed so much? Obviously, there have been advances in both technology and artificial intelligence. We can have virtual reality training. We digitize most paperwork these days. We have had advances in online learning. Strayer University, for example, has recruited Emmy-winning film producers for their online courses.[29] But another big reason is the streamlining of content—and new ways of thinking about that content.

As an example, for a long time, training in electronics focused on understanding a technical standard. But production staff really need to know the skills to do the job; the *how* of his job is more critical than the *why* behind every part of a standard.

Let's go back to the Uncle Buck example. Does he need to know why his nephew has decided to take tuba lessons? No. He just needs to get him there safely and soundly and pick him up when the lesson is over.

IPC's approach to stackable credentialing was acquiring the industry-supplied content and focusing on transforming it into instructional materials that would help new employees actually do their jobs. Part of developing this program was knowing *how* to teach so that the coursework reflected the best methodologies for learning. In general, you want to approach leaning from many different angles or modalities.

HOW DO WE LEARN?

I am sure you have had a conversation with a friend at some point when they said, "I am a visual learner," or "I am an audible learner," or "I need to be physically engaged to learn." Perhaps you've even said one of these statements yourself.

The latest research, however, shows that is not the case. This is a debunked theory; however, it persists, both in the classroom, from kindergarten on, as well as in corporate training and onboarding.[30]

The false belief in this myth means that for some, it is a self-fulfilling prophecy. People will say, "I can't learn that way," or "I can only learn by doing." Instead, when planning onboarding, those who design the instruction need to use as many modes as possible. By doing so, you'll activate as many different brain pathways as possible and make more connections. Making more connections improves memory.[31]

> *If you think about the very nature of life—I mean,*
> *in the very beginning, the development of the first*
> *cell divided into two cells—the sole purpose of*
> *life has been to pass on what was learned.*
> —MORGAN FREEMAN AS PROFESSOR NORMAN IN THE MOVIE *LUCY*

This concept is so important that you must make sure any system your company is purchasing is leveraging as many of those learning modalities as possible.

The Forgetting / Remembering Curve

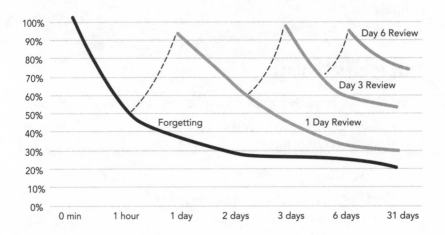

Figure 4.1: The science of forgetting

First, know that whatever you teach, there is going to be a certain amount of information forgotten. In fact, a *large* amount. Research on forgetting shows that within one hour of a presentation, people forget about half. Twenty-four hours later, they have forgotten about 70 percent of whatever new information you passed along in training. A week later, that climbs to 90 percent.[32] Though various studies may change the percentages, some people cite retaining 20 percent of what they hear, more for what they see, still higher for what they see *and* hear, and the highest percentage for what they do (hands-on learning).

This means that *blended* learning is the best. You hit as many ways to learn as possible. So if you review something within the first twenty-four hours of learning it, your chance of retention goes up. But if you reinforce it three days later, and then seven days later—then again thirty days later—this is the path to owning that information forever. Here's a fascinating look at retention.

Learners retain:

- ninety percent of what they learn when they teach someone else or use immediately,

- seventy-five percent of what they learn when they practice what they learned,

- fifty percent of what they learn when engaged in group discussions,

- thirty percent of what they learn when they see demonstrations,

- twenty percent of what they learn from audio-visual aids,

- ten percent of what they learn when they've learned from reading, and

- five percent of what they learn when they've learned from lectures.[33]

So let's look at how this might work in a credentialing program. Your new employee passes the test—great! But then shortly afterward, you might send them a couple of quiz questions via email that they have to answer. This "jogs" that memory and pulls up the information again. (And if they miss a question or two, you can send them the module pertaining to that concept, and they can engage with it again—because, remember, you are trying to have repeatable, consistent information retained.) You can do refreshers once a quarter. Then you do one again in six months. And now suddenly you have made your team smarter because you've kept the information fresh in their recall, and you refresh it periodically without overburdening them. No one wants to have to take a whole course again. This refreshing keeps it all in manageable chunks.

You want visual learning. You want aural learning. You want tactile learning. (For those who really want to go all out, there are other modes that can be engaged as well—more is better in the memory game.) In the era of online learning and materials, tactile learning is harder to accomplish. We need to keep innovating there.

How do you find these great learning modules? One place to start is trade associations particular to your industry. Check in with them to find out what they are doing on the workforce front and onboarding.

Consider the following when exploring an onboarding program:

- What are other industries doing? What about your own?

- How are your competitors certifying people? (Examples include programs like Cisco certification, in which a degree is not obtained—but certification is.)

- Does the program deliver the information your employees need to actually *do* their jobs?

- Who are the creators of the program? How many companies in your industry were involved in the creation?

- In terms of instructional design, how many different learning modalities does the program leverage?

- Which employees comprise the audience it's been geared toward—production staff, technicians, engineers, management, executives? *One size does not fit all.*

Look for simple solutions as well. If you are repeating certain training within your own company, why not record it? If you're going to use your greatest resources (your people) to do part of the training and educating, record it so they can do it just once. Aside from saving time, recording it means that everyone who views it gets the same consistent training.

At IPC we have a printing room, and it needed painting. I suggest painting one of the walls green—like the green screen. We record in there. Now we don't have to hang a backdrop. We have lights in there. When I do my monthly videos, it's lights, camera, action, roll the tape! (Just don't send a job to the printer for a few minutes!)

MY SHADOW AND ME

One way some companies onboard is shadowing. As I alluded to earlier, it uses your valuable resources (your people), when instead you should be looking for programs that cover a large percentage of onboarding that's generalizable in external programs.

Another aspect of shadowing as an onboarding methodology is that some people are amazingly good at their jobs. They just can't teach. I can think of one top school in the country where I had some business. The school had four Nobel Prize winning professors. However, that didn't make them good teachers.

In fact, often researchers just want to do research. In the same way, you may have employees who know everything there is about a certain position. But they are simply not cut out to guide a new hire.

Another program people talk about when onboarding is an apprenticeship. The words "apprenticeship" and "internship" are sometimes used interchangeably, but they are two different things. One way to think of it is that "an apprenticeship is work-based training, while an internship is work-based learning. While there are some similarities between internships and apprenticeships, the two are inherently different."[34]

The government even offers some incentives for the right kinds of apprenticeship programs. The problem is that your company is going to use valuable resources (again, your people) to train someone (usually from scratch), but there is no guarantee that at the end of the apprenticeship, they will even come work for you.

In addition, apprenticeships usually focus on a set of specific skills—a narrow lane. This may work for hands-on skill sets, but as knowledge workers increase, those types of jobs will become less adaptable to apprenticeship programs.

Internships often work for both parties. Your company has an opportunity to observe how the intern works and fits into the corporate culture. The intern obtains valuable experience—and to see if the company is a fit for them. Very often, internships result in job offers, particularly in certain industries.

DON'T FORGET YOUR CULTURE

We'll cover your corporate culture in chapter seven, but we must make some mention of it here. Let's go back to the definition of onboarding again: it involves the "skills, processes, knowledge, and behaviors" integral to coming aboard in your company. Let's look at that last item—behaviors. Do you welcome your employees in a way that makes them feel part of the team as soon as possible? Again, we'll discuss this in more detail later, but here are some points to consider:

- Make sure you emphasize your company's culture (things like diversity, commitment to community, the company mission) from the interview stage on. It's better for potential employees to know if they are a match on some of these fundamental elements or not.

- Provide informal networking opportunities. They should not all be happy hours, or all be sports events, or whatever it is.

The opportunities should include a variety of activities and events to be more inclusive.

- Communicate. Communicate. Communicate.

- Find ways to make new employees feel part of the team right away. This can be as simple as taking them out to lunch or walking them around and introducing them to everyone (not all at once, as that can be overwhelming).

- Make sure newbies know they can ask questions—and whom to ask.

- As you bring someone aboard, don't forget to clue them in on the little things as well as the big things: "Just so you know, our casual Friday is pretty laid back. You can wear jeans and T-shirts"; "We have a walking group during lunch hours. We'd love to have you join us"; "We have free gourmet coffee and snacks in the lunchroom." (Trust me, that coffee thing was a hit at IPC.)

KEY CONCEPTS

I've compiled a list of some best practices and ideas for knowledge transfer and onboarding (at least until we master the whole AI-information-transfer-to-the-brain thing).

- Take advantage of new technology. This can include online learning and virtual simulations.

- Avoid "death by PowerPoint." Make content as engaging as possible.

- Do not forget the "little things"—parts of your culture, such as how to dress or what people usually do on lunch hours, making sure the new employee knows their way around their surroundings and that they know whom to go to when they have questions.

- Find cost-effective programs for the repeatable elements that are *not* unique to your company.

- Do not tie up your best resources (your people) when standardized programs can do much of the work.

- Remember that not everyone is a teacher or trainer.

- Use documentation and manuals (online, not paper—don't kill more trees) for practices and onboarding that employees can easily refer to on their own as well as for the basics of benefits and employee policies (what used to be called orientation).

- Ensure your onboarding is consistent—not dependent on who your new employee's team leader is.

- Get people involved in hands-on ways where possible. Today's factories for top companies look *nothing* like the dark factory days of the 1960s or 1970s. This isn't the *I Love Lucy* episode with countless chocolates coming down a conveyer belt at high speed and Lucy and Ethel stuffing them in their mouths and under their hats. Artificial technology, the latest technology, and safer, cleaner, brighter workspaces are the norm. Production and technician positions can be ideal fits for many people. For example, older people should be part of your recruitment plan—today's factory jobs, with some cross-training, are far less physically demanding than walking miles and miles stocking shelves in a big-box factory or warehouse.

- Make sure you are utilizing the latest research on retention and learning. Use tactile, visual, and aural methodologies. Repeat information in manageable chunks.

- Shadowing and apprenticeships are rarely effective. Internships are.

- Ensure that employees can refresh their skills. Utilize solutions like filming repeatable onboarding elements so that employees can go back and access them at any time.

Next we'll move on to discussing what happens once your employee is fully on board—pathways and upskilling.

ACME VERSUS NEW CO.

If you are not familiar with "Acme" in the world of Looney Tunes cartoons, it was the company from which Wile E. Coyote ordered all of his destructive equipment to try to eliminate his arch nemesis, the Road Runner. When you see these sections, Acme will represent how a company has "always done things." New Co. will be, as its name suggests, the company in which the ideas in this book are represented in a fictional way. In the final chapter of the book, you will see some examples from real-life companies embracing these ideas of the future (and, as we'll see repeatedly in this book, the future is now).

⊗ ACME'S ONBOARDING STYLE

Tom, the new engineer, has come aboard with a degree, a charming personality, smarts—but no experience and zero practical skills. On his first day, the human resources director goes over his healthcare package and company holidays and has him fill out his direct deposit form and other digitized paperwork. The HR director notices he is dressed in a suit and tie when everyone else in the company prefers khakis and polo shirts—business casual attire. She doesn't say anything. She also fails to mention the company's latest "volunteer day" and the charity Acme has decided to focus on. If the company has a mission statement, it's not a part of that first day.

The HR director's assistant walks him to his cubicle, logs him onto a computer, and directs him to hours' worth of online training modules. She tells Tom to complete them in order until his department head can bring him in to go over more of what he will be doing. The modules are old and poorly produced, and several times each module requires rewinding to try to catch what is being said. He needs coffee. Now. But he has no idea where it is. For that matter, he's not even sure where the restrooms are.

Acme's best engineer, a director hired by the CEO himself, is dynamic, has a wealth of experience, and is a knowledge keeper. In fact, Ellen Engineer's so good that no one understands why she hasn't moved up to the next level. Her salary is the highest in her department. However, anytime a new employee comes aboard, she handles the training. Because she stores so much content in her head, it has not been added to the company training modules—or any document. If Ellen ever leaves the company, that information will walk out the door with her. She keeps getting pinged on LinkedIn by recruiters.

While Ellen really should be concentrating on the major new product introduction that is coming, instead she must sit down with Tom on his second day and give him an hourlong rundown of the department. She is interrupted by three phone calls.

"Any questions, just come find me," she says. "My door is always open." However, Tom senses she is one more deadline shy of pulling out her hair.

Stressed about the new launch and the report she needs to give to the CEO by end of day Friday, she smiles warmly but says she really must attend to the crises on her desk. Ellen brings Tom to her direct-report engineer, David Data, who prefers computers to humans but is great at data analysis. Tom is assured that Ellen will "circle back" so he can ask questions and discuss his experiences at the end of the day and assures him he is in "good hands" with David. Both are incorrect.

Tom knows about the team's deadline now, and he feels guilty bothering the director to ask questions—but he can't even locate her anyway. He knows he *has* questions, but he feels so lost and overwhelmed that he's not even sure where to start.

David briefly explains to Tom what he will be doing—but he doesn't *show* him any of it. "The online modules explain it all," he assures him and walks him back to his cubicle. It's now noon, and Tom's hungry, but no one's told him how long his lunch hour actually is or when it officially starts. It's day two, and he still doesn't know where the break room and cafeteria are. He finds a vending machine and eats Doritos at his desk.

Soon, Tom is frustrated because he's unsure of what he should be doing. He's confused by the program that everyone is using in house to populate various forms and processes. Ellen, still having no time to rectify this, passes him along to Mark, whose secret nickname among the team is "Mark the Micromanager." Tom doesn't know which is worse: knowing nothing about what he is supposed to do or having Mark want to approve and see every single thing he does. Twice.

It takes Tom six months until he's even baseline *competent* at his job.

⊘ NEW CO.'S NEW WAY: ONBOARDING

Nadine, the new engineer, has come aboard with a degree, a charming personality, and smarts—but no experience and zero practical skills. Fortunately, she is very excited for her first day at New Co. Several people on her team have already reached out to her via LinkedIn. Three people have already asked her to join them for a "first day" lunch at a nearby restaurant, an unspoken company tradition. The restaurant offers vegan selections as well as other fare, and it's one where someone can find something on the menu, no matter their dietary requirements—a reason it is a popular favorite at New Co.

She has already filled out much of her paperwork before she even started. She has read through several modules and has been given an already populated calendar of things to learn, meetings, etc., for her first thirty, sixty, and ninety days.

On her first day, the HR director goes over her healthcare package via a well-produced video. Her direct deposit form and other digitized paperwork have already been taken care of, so the first-day HR inter-action is more about checking in with Nadine to see if she has any questions. Nadine has arrived in business casual—her boss had already let her know via LinkedIn that dress is business casual except on Fridays, when jeans are the norm and the company provides lunch for everyone to team build.

The HR director's assistant walks Nadine to her cubicle. It has already been set up, complete with a nameplate, a welcome basket of snacks, a note from her direct supervisor, and access to the computer system. Her supervisor comes over the moment she sees Nadine, greets her warmly, and takes her to meet the team in her surrounding area.

When her supervisor walks her back to her cubicle, they load up a module for her on some of the aspects of the computer system she needs to know. Nadine is told to let her supervisor know when she has completed the first two modules so that they can talk through any questions. Nadine does so and is reassured when the conversation with her supervisor is warm, friendly, and reassuring.

"Any questions, just come find me," her boss says. "My door is always open." As Nadine observes the way the office works, she realized that her boss's door really *is* always open, and there is a strong sense of team in the area.

One of her coworkers, who has been working for New Co. for two years now, comes over and says he has been assigned to take her through the building to see more of the company's operations. He walks her through the break room and cafeteria, points out the bathrooms, shows her a lounge area where people are free to work on their laptops in a more relaxed environment, walks her through the company lending library and a nondenominational prayer room should she wish to take time to meditate, and along the way, he introduces her to several people they pass in the hallways.

At lunch, she is filled in more on some of the fun things the company does for its employees as part of its team building, including a yearly family picnic. Her new coworkers also let her know more about the volunteer efforts for this quarter: collecting children's books for a local children's hospital's library.

After lunch, she makes her way through two more modules. Then her boss calls her in for some more informal discussion of the job before she is given a brief online test on the modules she worked through. Before Nadine knows it, it's nearly five o'clock. Her boss stops by her workspace and says, "By the way, we do sometimes work late at crunch time, but we very much believe in work-life balance here. Please don't feel like you need to stay late—no one is asking for that. We give a heads-up if we foresee any overtime, and we try to give enough warning that arrangements can be made if you need to adjust your plans. See you tomorrow! Hope you had a great day. Remember, we truly want you to feel like part of New Co.!"

PATHWAYS AND UPSKILLING

Growing Your Employees

---

*It's supposed to be hard. If it wasn't hard, everyone
would do it. The hard is what makes it great.*
—A LEAGUE OF THEIR OWN

PATHWAYS: FOLLOW THE YELLOW BRICK ROAD

James L. Ziemer rode his first Harley-Davidson "hog" at age fifteen
and had an early fascination with motorcycles. He started work at
Harley-Davidson as a freight elevator operator. Over a three-decade
career, he moved to accounting, eventually working his way to chief
operating officer and then finally CEO.[35] Mary Barra, of General
Motors fame, started out inspecting fenders when she was eighteen.

She worked her way up to become the first female CEO of a major automaker.[36]

Pathways, as you may recall from our definition in chapter one, take an employee from a job to a career. Pathways are the roadmaps to advancement and growth along a career path and a desired future position. Like streetlights on a dark road, they illuminate just where to go.

Not everyone is a Mary Barra or a James Ziemer. Some people may be aiming for the C-suite. Some in the C-suite may want the CEO spot; others may be looking to be team leads. But regardless of their levels of ambition, the majority of your employees want to know that they have an actual career path to follow. Let's say you graduated as an English major, and you joined a major publishing company. You may start out reading through the "slush pile" of manuscripts sent in by the thousands. That's a lot of (mostly) bad books to read through. It's boring and it's tedious. It's a start—but it's not where you want to *stay*. It's important for you to know there is an actual career progression to follow from this entry-level job to junior editor, to editor, to senior editor, to director of a publishing imprint, and so on.

Here's an example from my own experiences. After I joined IPC, I visited many factories across China. IPC is a global leader with over three hundred active multilingual industry standards, covering nearly every stage of the electronics product development cycle. There are more than five thousand electronic industry professionals participating in the development of these standards globally. Therefore, it's important for me to be informed about what is going on across the world.

In China, the headcount turnover is extremely high. It is reported as 20 to 30 percent of their workforce in manufacturing,[37] but talking with line managers, I've found that it's likely much higher. In North

America, that would be viewed as a catastrophe. Basically, that number means that every two to three years, you have an entirely new workforce.

I was taking tours at numerous facilities, and I was trying to understand the challenges of the industry there. And the big challenge coming up consistently was turnover. *How do we keep people? They're always moving. If we train them, they go away. Why should we spend money to train them? They're just going to go get a job across the street for more money.*

Then I visited a particular North American company's factory in China. I assumed they faced this same problem. So I asked what their turnover rate was. They informed me it was lower than 10 percent. I immediately was curious: "What are you doing that is different from some of your peers and competitors?"

One might assume that it was about more money (you know the adage about "never assume," right?). In fact, raising wages does not combat turnover in China.[38]

What about better facilities? Nope. Though their facility was modern and a nice place to work, so were the other electronics factories near them. So that wasn't it.

So I looked at their situation in more depth. They had a *similar* pathway as others. With one very big difference. If we use the tried and true analogy of climbing the ladder of success, they had much shorter rungs. Every four to eight weeks, employees could get little promotions.

Thus, people at this factory could think: "If I stay here, and I learn these things and these skills, then I can become a level two at this position in four weeks. Then in another six weeks, I can move to this position. And then in another four weeks, I could be at this level if I work hard."

At each level, they are learning new skills and being challenged. I looked around and noticed that they had these levels depicted visually on charts on the walls. Every day, employees know exactly how they could become the supervisor—and more importantly, that it was really *possible*. They could see their peers moving up within the company.

> **Every day, employees know exactly how they could become the supervisor—and more importantly, that it was really possible. They could see their peers moving up within the company.**

They created a system with shorter and shorter rewards. Certain employees—for example, demographically younger workers—are motivated by seeing what they can become and how high they can advance.[39] For older workers who might be close to retirement, the position title might not mean as much as far as their pathway, but they also know raises are built into that structure.

So the lesson is that the more clearly you can spell out the pathway, the more motivating it is for your employees. You, of course, want to hire a great person right off the bat. But that great person is great *because* they are ambitious and want to do more—they want to find their challenges and their passions.

In fact, the pathways issue is one of the big challenges of being a smaller organization like IPC. If one of my C-suite VPs says to me, "John, in five years, I want to be CEO," in five years I still plan to be in that office position—which means if that is their ambition, they will likely have to leave and find that elsewhere. And that's OK.

I am a firm believer that you want the very best people for what they can bring to the fabric of your company, even if their ultimate dreams are beyond that path you have outlined. Remember that today's younger employees change positions more frequently than employees of other generations (see figure 5.1).

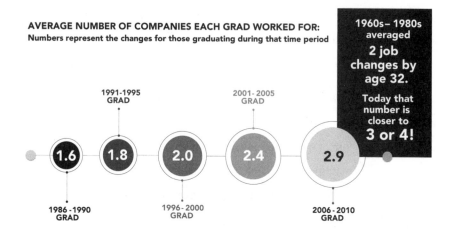

Figure 5.1: Job changes by age demographics[40]

You may recall from the previous chapter that today's generation of workers has a more negative view of manufacturing than when we were in the "olden days" discussed in chapter one. In fact, 45 percent of younger workers have a negative perception of manufacturing jobs.[41]

Some of the reasons for that are outdated notions of what working in today's manufacturing jobs is really like. But a big reason is the myth that a factory job is a dead-end career path. We must work to dispel this myth to help alleviate the perceived "worker shortage."

There are many positives to today's manufacturing jobs. These include the following:

- Cutting-edge technology. Drones, 3-D printing, artificial intelligence … if today's generation is tech oriented, then today's factories offer a whole new world to them, a chance to be working on and with game-changing technology.

- Increased safety and better facilities. Too many of us still picture windowless, grimy factories in pictures and movies and miniseries about early factory work in the building of America (or other countries). I wish I could take every reader on a tour of some IPC members' facilities.

- Factory jobs that are not on the floor. To run these facilities, companies need all kinds of workers—from accountants to programmers to sales to marketing. We need to get the message out—don't dismiss manufacturing as a career just because you are a knowledge worker.

- Entry-level positions, on-the-job training, *pathways,* and leadership opportunities. Manufacturing is a great place to grow a career.

- Being part of *building* something. Pride in creating something.

We need to dismiss the myths about manufacturing. Clear pathways will help that.

UPSKILLING: FILLING THE SKILLS GAP

Upskilling tends to be viewed hand in hand with pathways. Remember our definition from chapter one: *Upskilling is adding new capabilities relevant to changes in the industry or additional skills needed to enhance capabilities.*

Let me give you an example. Let's say I'm an engineer. And I happen to design monitors. Terrific. We used to make those one way, but now there's artificial intelligence. AI is going to help me create this new type of modern monitor—in record speed too. Unfortunately, I don't know anything about artificial intelligence. I don't know anything about data analytics—that wasn't part of my curriculum.

I need a new skill—that's upskilling. It's giving me more tools in my toolbox. It is helping me grow with the changes in my industry.

The tricky thing is those tools are constantly changing. Remember Moore's law? Gordon Moore, the cofounder of Intel, theorized that "the number of transistors on a microchip doubles every two years, though the cost of computers is halved. Moore's law states that we can expect the speed and capability of our computers to increase every couple of years, and we will pay less for them. Another tenet of Moore's law asserts that this growth is exponential."[42]

> I need a new skill—that's upskilling. It's giving me more tools in my toolbox. It is helping me grow with the changes in my industry.

Artificial intelligence is also growing, as these statistics from a *Harvard Business Review* article illuminate:

- In a recent study, 86 percent of companies surveyed believe artificial intelligence is now mainstream technology.

- Almost three-quarters of business leaders (72 percent) feel positively about the role that AI will play in the future. (Clearly they have never seen *I, Robot.*)

- Seventy-four percent of executives not only anticipate that AI will make their business processes more efficient, but they also believe it will help create new business models (55 percent) and will lead to new products and services/innovations (54 percent).[43]

We also should not fear AI as far as jobs and employment. Unfortunately, this myth perpetuates, as people fear robots will replace them. However, that's not the full story: "In its *Future of Jobs Report 2020*, the World Economic Forum estimates that 85 million jobs will be displaced while 97 million new jobs will be created across 26 countries by 2025."[44]

However, these changes mean that upskilling is required—and it must be refreshed constantly. As you can see in figure 5.2, we have a lot of new knowledge to absorb.

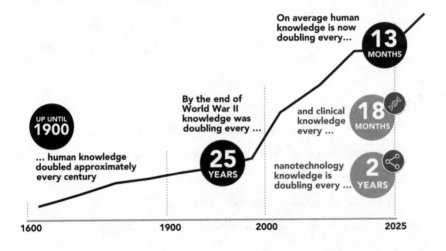

Figure 5.2: The knowledge-doubling curve[45]

However, upskilling is not only the vision of robotic arms, 3-D printing, and sci-fi-like technology. Upskilling can include all different skills. Some real-world examples include the following:

- Upskilling a language differential

- Upskilling a stylistic differential

- Learning to type faster or more efficiently with a different keyboard layout (such as Dvorak or Colemak) instead of QWERTY

- Learning how to use a word processor

- Being promoted from within, learning new skills and responsibilities in a new position—or even in the same department, or leading a team for the first time

- Attending a coding workshop

- Using virtual course platforms to learn new skills

- Online learning of both hard and soft skills—for example, using Lynda.com (acquired by LinkedIn to create LinkedIn Learning)

RESISTANCE TO CHANGE

We also need to recognize that there are people who want to learn new skills and follow that "ladder," as shown in the China-based factory I mentioned earlier. But there are also people who will be very resistant to change. They may be perfectly content where they are. That *might* be OK in a static position that never changes.

But as we've demonstrated, that's a very rare thing these days. Today's employee needs to be someone who is *willing* to continue to learn. Notice that I said *willing to*. If they're not willing to continue to learn, sometimes it's in both your best interests to part ways. With the advances in technology, we can all grow together!

Human skill development in any nation is key
for economic growth.
—LAILAH GIFTY AKITA, FOUNDER, SMART YOUTH VOLUNTEERS FOUNDATION

I'm going to give an example from my own experience. At one company I was working at, a woman in a key administrative assistant position had been there for a dozen years. She was in a professional rut—and very closed to learning the new technology we were bringing aboard. Consequently, she was unhappy, and that bled into how she interacted with others.

When all our efforts to offer upskilling failed, I knew we needed to let her go. When we informed her that we needed to part ways, something happened that I had never encountered before. She was *happy.* Perhaps it was a relief to be let go from a job she no longer felt matched her skill set.

The point is that you can't *make* someone upskill. It is essential that your coworkers be willing to evolve their capabilities.

RESKILLING

In July of 2019, Amazon made a reskilling pledge. The giant will spend $700 million dollars on retraining 100,000 of its workers.[46] The retraining will focus on new skills needed with automation and artificial intelligence changes.

"Reskilling" is sometimes used interchangeably with "upskilling." The difference is, generally, that reskilling is a pivot. It's a totally different skill, not advancing the skills you already have.

Here are some real-world examples:

- A warehouse receiver learns to repair robotic arms.

- A stocker is retrained to do order capture.

- A retail worker at a closing bricks-and-mortar store reskills to be an online customer support specialist.

- An accountant reskills to become a data analyst.

UPSKILLING STRATEGIES

As I noted, upskilling must constantly be refreshed. The time to upskill is not two years down the line when your employees' skills are completely antiquated. It needs to be ongoing. So what are the strategies for keeping people challenged and developing in the workplace?

First, you want to be giving the people you work with new projects, engaging them in different things, allowing them to make a difference. Remember—money is not the sole motivator for people. Feeling engaged is essential. In fact, according to a Gallup poll, here are five things employees say they want in their next job:[47]

1. **BETTER WORK-LIFE BALANCE.** As we discussed earlier, the "Great Reprioritization" brought about by the global COVID-19 pandemic has caused people to rethink their jobs, especially in the area of balance.

2. **THE ABILITY TO DO WHAT THEY EXCEL AT.** There's that "passion" motivation.

3. **GREAT STABILITY AND JOB SECURITY.** This includes looking to the future. Does your company have a growth plan that your employees can believe in?

4. **INCREASED BENEFITS OR INCOME.** While people will make lateral switches sometimes in order to leave toxic

environments, most people don't want to go through all of the change and adaptation for exactly what they have now.

5. **DIVERSITY AND INCLUSIVENESS.** We will cover these in the next chapter.

As an example, at one of the companies where I worked, the board highlighted to me at one point that the customer experience at the organization could be improved. It was good—we wanted *great*. I decided that instead of just asking the VP of that division to go analyze the team and fix it, we needed to hear from the actual people who were going to be part of this upskilling of our customer service. I invited lower-level employees—at least four levels below my CEO position—from every single division. I created and led a cross-functional team. All of a sudden, these people had this huge responsibility. I said, "You are responsible for understanding all the issues that your division sees from your perspective."

We will be discussing diversity in the next chapter. But I made sure we had every possible cohort. We had a whole different set of age groups, different sets of experience, different backgrounds. But just assembling this team was not enough.

This team was *empowered* because they knew they were going be listened to—because they had the CEO running it. Think of your own experiences. I am sure you have had times in your career when great shows were made of forming teams to make "change." And nothing ever was done with the findings.

I think that for some of the people on the team, it felt a little strange or scary to be giving ideas to the CEO. But, as I always try to do, I made sure they knew that I valued their opinions. And it also was enriching for me. I got to learn about these dozen people and their talents.

Speaking of talents, skills assessments should be part of upskilling. You can't know what new skills are needed if you don't know where you are starting from.

WHAT IF YOU UPSKILL YOUR EMPLOYEES INTO ... LEAVING YOU?

What happens if you put all this time and effort into upskilling, and your employee takes those skills and ... takes off? As I shared in my travels to China, this all too often is a concern I hear from management in many parts of the world: "What if they leave?"

Three things. First, while that will happen, if you are motivating your employees right, if you are showing them the *pathway* those new skills will open in their career with *you,* if they feel valued, it shouldn't be something you worry about. Valued employees are more loyal, and *that* provides great returns—well beyond the investment in their improvement.[48]

Two, you actually don't have a choice. You need to keep your workforce abreast of the changes and skill sets needed in their industry. Otherwise, they—and you—will be left behind in this competitive environment.

The third is a story. I was at a leadership conference, and a successful coach of the Utah Valley University basketball team, Mark Pope, was giving the keynote. As much as I like basketball, I was kind of puzzled and wondered what Coach Pope was going to say to us.

He told of how his team was an underdog. But they started beating many of the teams in the state, almost out of nowhere. This included the big schools with big basketball programs. He said that yes, he had a team with a lot of talent. But he attributed much of their success to the talent of the coaching staff. And he had an interesting philosophy, which he shared. He basically said (I'm paraphrasing), "Look, I'm here to grow my coaching staff to get them the best coaching jobs they can. I want them to go to Kentucky. I want them to go to NC State. I want them to coach in the NBA. I want them to go here and there—and they know that. So they're going to give me their best because they know I'm trying to get them in better jobs than I have."

Coach Pope's thinking has relevance to our pathways and upskilling discussion. That sort of approach and philosophy coming from your organization shows employees—and potential employees—that your organization is going to invest in their people and make them the best possible. Yes, they may leave at some point. But as we discussed in chapter one, today's people aren't lifers.

And I have a philosophy that a no today might one day be a yes when I recruit people. And by the same token, someone may leave my company as they upskill. Who knows? One day they might be back. I experienced this during my time working at Bose. I have never seen so many people who had come back to a company after trying out somewhere else.

Deal with the fact that people may leave if you give them new skills. If you get three years out of them, and they're really good employees, you probably made a gold mine on them (especially if they are in senior positions). But they just may show superior loyalty because yours is a forward-thinking company that believes in and invests in them.

KEY CONCEPTS

- Pathways demonstrate to your employees that they have future paths with your company.

- Pathways transform jobs to careers.

- Pathways should have short rungs where possible, especially on the manufacturing floor. Let your employees see their progress.

- The top motivator for people is not always money (though money is part of it). Growth and passion are important too.

- Upskilling helps to solve some of your pipeline issues. Rather than parting ways with a good employee, grow them into a new position or new skills.

- Reskilling is a pivot to a completely new job type.

- Upskilling may lead people to other jobs, but in today's employment environment, that's OK.

- Know where current skills are through assessments.

ACME AND NEW CO.'S PATHWAYS AND UPSKILLING

✖ ACME'S APPROACH

Eddie Valiant, Acme's customer service manager, is interviewing Jessica Rabbit for their open customer service position. He explains the shift she would be working, along with the types of calls she would be handling.

After giving her a rundown of Acme's patented jet-propulsion pogo stick—a market Acme has cornered, along with their anvil division—Eddie goes over the basic benefits package.

Ms. Rabbit, a fan of Acme's rocket-powered roller skates, is excited to perhaps be part of the Acme organization. She is also pleased that employees get a 10 percent discount on Acme products. She is excited to be part of such a well-known organization. The benefits are great—she's making a move from freelancing, so those are very important to her.

Ms. Rabbit inquires, "So is there room for advancement? What would that look like?"

Eddie Valiant smiles and says, "We offer two dollars an hour more than Anvils-R-Us. But really, customer service is sort of its own area. There's one supervisor, who has been here fifteen years. And then there's me."

Meanwhile, in research and development, Acme's best engineer is having his annual review. Once again, the review is stellar. There is nothing Marvin Mensa can't do, and he has met or exceeded every single key performance indicator (KPI) his vice president has set for him. He is given a decent raise above the cost of living, indicating how pleased Acme is to have him aboard, along with verbal kudos. However, once again, there are no ambitious goals to reach because there is not a visible pathway into upper management. All of Acme's products sell very well, but they are no longer innovating, and Marvin feels his creativity slipping away. He spends time at home advancing his skills via some online learning platforms, with an eye to perhaps jumping ship to New Co., one of their competitors.

On the top floor in the C-suite, Mr. W. E. Coyote is interviewing a potential new senior manager in the Anvil Compliance Department. Mr. Jones's résumé is an *exact* fit for the position.

"I'd really like to grow with my position. There is also an upper-level certification at Barnett College. I'd be interested in that and to see where I can go. I think every anvil company is going to be moving toward these new standards."

"While I appreciate that," CEO Coyote says, "and we can look into it, we really need you to focus on the issues we currently have before we start thinking about the future."

"Sure, but speaking of future, I do want you to know that I am passionate about jet propulsion. My master's thesis was on it, and I had the good fortune to study with R. Runner. Perhaps you've heard of him?"

"Yes, but anvil compliance has been having issues filling positions as well as regulatory problems. We need someone like you. Compliance is the ideal fit for you. I don't know that jet propulsion would be a direction I'd point you."

They talk more, and Mr. Jones is offered the position. However, if he comes aboard Acme, he will be doing the *exact same thing* he does in his current position for a 15 percent increase in salary.

⊘ NEW CO.'S NEW INNOVATIONS

New Co.'s HR manager reaches out to Marvin Mensa, a top engineer at Acme, to see if he might like to interview for a key position at New Co. He jumps at the chance, and after a preliminary interview with HR, he is passed along to the senior vice president of quality assurance. When he inquires about future growth, he is told, "That is one of the reasons we are so interested in you. Your background is a perfect fit—but we have some innovations we'd love to implement. We think you could be instrumental in helping us. More than that, this position would give you more responsibility, and we would like to see you move into upper management within a year once you learn the ropes here. We think you could have a bright future here."

Meanwhile, five new production employees are going through their orientation. Their supervisor meets with them and then points out, "Right now, we're starting you on the line. But after ninety days, if you are interested, you can be trained on how to program and repair our robotic arms. That is a level II production worker—and there is a raise associated with that. After *that,* in six months, you could become a technician team leader. We promote from within, so from there, you could be an operations manager or a field service technician supervisor." She shows them a flow chart, and on it are listed the various pay grades for each position. "The sky is the limit here at New Co. We reward talent, hard work, and ambition." At the end of the orientation, she brings in the vice president of purchasing. He shares with the new employees that he started out in their very position. He took advantage of the company's generous paid education for certifications, and he details how he rose within the company.

CHAPTER SIX

DIVERSITY AND INCLUSION

Making Room for Everyone

> *But in times of crisis the wise build bridges,*
> *while the foolish build barriers.*
> —*BLACK PANTHER*

Diverse teams always give better decisions.

Always.

There are many reasons for this. When we share ideas with freedom to be authentic, with openness, and with a wide variety of perspectives and experiences, we arrive at stronger outcomes.

One reason for this has to do with the theory in James Surowiecki's seminal book, *The Wisdom of Crowds: Why the Many Are Smarter Than the Few and How Collective Wisdom Shapes Business, Economies, Societies, and Nations*. In his work, Surowiecki posits that a group of diverse people will make a better decision than a handful of brilliant elite thinkers. According to the author, the wisdom of crowds depends on five elements:[49]

1. **DIVERSITY OF OPINION**

2. **INDEPENDENCE**

3. **DECENTRALIZATION**

4. **AGGREGATION**

5. **TRUST (THAT THE GROUP WILL BE FAIR)**

I've seen this proven time and time again. A story I like to tell is from when I was in graduate school. We needed to form groups for our major project—one that would really determine our grade. I was selected to create all the teams. At that I stepped back and looked at my classmates. I was a white male of a certain age, with certain experiences. I didn't think the project would be better for being composed of people who looked, thought, and acted like me and had the same experiences that I had. Instead, I intentionally created the most diverse teams possible—for the whole class. While, admittedly, in graduate school, my cohorts were all educated people, which is one playing field, our teams were composed of different genders, ages, races, religions, geographies, and backgrounds.

And we excelled. In visiting and discussing with subsequent cohorts in which this kind of approach was *not* taken, the opposite was the case. Truly frustrating experiences were the result.

I am grateful to have, early in my career, learned that lesson. Diversity and inclusion better us all. In this chapter, we're not only going to discuss diversity and inclusion but also why these concepts are so important and valuable.

WHAT IS DIVERSITY?

Let's start with a good definition of workplace diversity:

> Diversity is defined by who we are as individuals.... [Our] strength comes from the dedication, experience, talents, and perspectives of every employee. Diversity encompasses the range of similarities and differences each individual brings to the workplace, including but not limited to national origin, language, race, color, disability, ethnicity, gender, age, religion, sexual orientation, gender identity, socioeconomic status, veteran status, and family structures. We define workforce diversity as a collection of individual attributes that together help us pursue organizational objectives efficiently and effectively.[50]

The belonging you seek is not behind you ... it is ahead.
—MAZ KANATA, *STAR WARS: THE LAST JEDI*

Sometimes people try to define diversity and inclusion in narrower terms, but diversity is a much bigger umbrella than that. It is not just ethnicity or gender or race or sexual orientation. It's also not enough for companies to say that they embrace diversity and inclusion. Like all the best actionable ideals, there must be measurement.

Companies must *live* the principles.

Let's look at some of the ambitions of the car giant Volvo, for example:

- By 2030, the automaker wants to achieve a level of 35 percent women in leadership. They call this #BreaktheBias.[51]

- Volvo—along with over fifty other European industrial and technology companies—has signed a pledge to #Embrace-Difference (an initiative by the European Round Table of Industrialists), a forum bringing together around fifty-five chief executives and chairpersons of major multinational companies. Embrace Difference targets "inclusive leadership, aspiration and goal setting, clear responsibility, equal opportunities, and societal engagement and responsibility."[52]

The US Intellectual Property Alliance has offered its own diversity pledge addressing the gender gap and other diversity issues in the area of innovation and invention. Companies that signed this pledge include AT&T, Dropbox, Facebook, HP, HPE, Lenovo, LinkedIn, Lumentum, Microsoft, NetApp, Nielsen, PayPal, P&G, SAP, Seagate Technology, Twilio, Uber, and others.[53]

What are the elements of diversity pledges? The CEO Action Pledge for Diversity and Inclusion has four parts:[54]

1. Continuing to make workplaces a place of trust, where complex and sometimes difficult conversations about diversity and inclusion are held

2. Implementing and expanding unconscious bias education

3. Sharing best practices and unsuccessful experiences

4. Creating and sharing strategic inclusion and diversity plans with the board of directors

This particular four-pronged CEO diversity pledge involves more than two thousand CEOs from large companies (e.g., 3M, Twenty-First Century Fox, Accenture, and Walmart).

WHY DIVERSITY IS SO IMPORTANT—AND WHY IT MAKES YOUR COMPANY BETTER

Now that we have defined diversity and know it is something global companies are declaring important to their future, we ask: Why is that?

I'm going to give you, in my own opinion, one of the most important reasons: *When people are free to show up as their most authentic selves, not needing to hide important aspects of who they are, they bring their very best energy, creativity, ideas, intellect, and work ethic to your organization.*

> **When people are free to show up as their most authentic selves, not needing to hide important aspects of who they are, they bring their very best energy, creativity, ideas, intellect, and work ethic to your organization.**

If this is not important to your company—you need to *Fire Your Hiring Habits* and assess.

Other important reasons include the following:

- Talent, part one. Today, diversity and inclusion are important to most workers. Glassdoor conducted a survey showing that an astonishing 67 percent of job seekers say that diversity and inclusion are some of the leading factors when they analyze job offers and employers.[55] You will simply not attract the best of today's talent unless your workplace embraces diversity. The world is moving forward—your company should be too.

- Talent, part two. Embracing diversity widens your talent pool from which to draw candidates. By following narrow, less diverse pipelines, you have fewer potential candidates.

- Diversity is good for your bottom line—your financials. A large-scale study was conducted of seventeen hundred companies in eight countries. Those with higher scores in diversity had higher innovation revenues.[56]

- Diverse teams arrive at better decisions (as James Surowiecki has informed us). A diverse team offers perspectives from a wide variety of backgrounds.

- Keeping your talent. Those on diverse teams are less likely to leave your organization. In fact, those on diverse teams are 19 percent more likely to stay with your organization.[57]

- Diversity drives innovation by inviting input from a much broader base of experiences and ideas.

If you don't believe me, here are some quotes from business leaders who feel that diversity and inclusion are essential for now and the future.

- Tim Cook, CEO of Apple, has said, "I think the most diverse group will produce the best product."[58]

- "A diverse mix of voices leads to better discussions, decisions, and outcomes for everyone," according to Sundar Pichai.[59]

- Jason Saltzman, founder and CEO of Alley, has stated, "One of the reasons many organizations struggle is because they look at culture and diversity as a product. They're taking a progressive notion of inclusion and turning it into something to sell. If this sounds familiar, don't pat yourself on the back simply for implementing diverse hiring practices. True diversity should be about empathy, not a part of your sales funnel."[60]

- Karen Horting, executive director and CEO of the Society of Women Engineers, sums it up: "Diversity is not an issue that just affects minorities or women. Diversity is an issue that affects the entire workforce."[61]

AXES OF DIVERSITY

Ideally you will try to bring together diversity from as many axes as possible. Go back to our diversity definition, and see how many areas inclusion impacts.

There's a famous story about the US Air Force building airplanes in the 1940s. The planes kept crashing—only it wasn't the planes themselves. Pilots kept losing control, and this was a puzzle. They were well trained. The planes were getting better and better as far as aerodynamics. So why couldn't the pilots keep them in the air?

The puzzle wasn't solved until the 1950s. I also want to specifically point out that the man who found the solution was twenty-three years old—and a pair of fresh eyes. Looking at the problem from a new perspective, he realized that when the cockpits were first being designed in the 1920s, the average height of men was used. The seats, reaches to buttons, etc. were positioned for that average height; not only that, but even the controls were designed for smaller hands. These averages used were compared to the actual pilot data—just about no one was the average. In situations with fighter pilots in which the most minute elements had to be perfect because of the intensity of the situation, these elements were literally causing pilots to die. Lockheed then realized they needed the seats customizable, among other things.[62]

This story is a reminder that diversity can take many things into consideration. There is no such thing as an average human being. We are a broad range of humanity.

Diversity should include levels of education as well. As I've said, I am certification oriented. I like company-wide teams to include those who've gone a little past high school and those who have advanced degrees so that we get perspectives from a variety of educational backgrounds.

Going back to our definition, you want to try to encompass the breadth of people and their uniqueness. It is essential that your company actively pursues this, taking the lead. We cannot fix all of society's problems regarding prejudice, economic disparities, systemic racism, gender inequities, homophobia, etc. But those of us who *can* impact our company's decisions have an obligation to be as inclusive as possible. It's sound business. And the right thing to do.

AGE IS JUST A NUMBER

When you think of diversity, go back to the definition at the beginning of our chapter. Diversity encompasses an entire expanse of areas. One that doesn't always spring to mind immediately is age.

I'm going to offer some personal examples. I was working at Bose, and we were hiring a brand-new team. We had younger candidates who were full of excitement. I admired their "We can conquer the world" and "Change is good" mentalities. They embraced new ideas. But at the same time, I am grateful I'd had the foresight to talk to the recruiter and request that they help me find someone who was either near retirement or recently retired as part of the leadership team, because that person would be able to see things from a career of experience and a different point of view.

At IPC, we were trying to improve our customer interactions, so I had someone from every single division. It was a team of about a dozen people. That team had diversity of division, but among them, I made sure we had diversity of gender, diversity of age, and diversity of experience.

One of the men on that team had been with IPC for a few decades. He was able to provide perspective on the changes over the years as to what had worked in the past and what had not. The younger members of the team were able to look at what we were trying to accomplish with a modern, fresh eye *with* the benefit of experience that the gentleman brought to the table.

> *If your rationale for doing something is "This is the way we've always done things," I assume you no longer want to work for me.*
> —JOHN MITCHELL (THAT'S ME!)

My other story has to do with being aware of your blind spots when it comes to working with other generations. I was taking a one-on-one meeting with a young woman on one of my teams. We were having what I thought was a positive conversation, but at some point during it, she began looking at her phone and typing furiously into it. From my perspective this was very odd—even disrespectful.

However, as I paid more attention in meetings to the younger employees, I noticed the same behavior. As it turns out, younger employees have no recollection of the Rolodex, of the Blackberry, of laptops that weighed forty-two pounds, or of cell phones the sizes and weights of bricks. What they *have* been part of is new generations of employees who have only known the technological advances we enjoy. Our phones have become ubiquitous. They carry our lives on them. Which is why this "disrespectful" behavior on the part of my employees turned out to be them taking notes on their phone—just the opposite of what I thought. They were actually trying to capture information.

The danger, of course, is that we are all capable of misinterpreting behaviors based on our own experiences. Diversity and inclusion benefit us all by exposing us to a variety of habits, behaviors, and ideas across multiple cohorts.

The workplace is changing. As of 2020, 62 percent of millennials said they have direct reports.[63] As you may recall earlier in the book, there are some generalities we might make about the attributes, expectations, and views toward work by generation.

GENDER DIVERSITY

Women still make up only roughly 25 percent of the C-suite. Even more disheartening, women make up only 17 percent of the CEOs in the Fortune 500.[64]

Certain industries are even worse:

- When Jane Fraser took over as CEO of Citi in 2021, she was the *first* woman to head a major US bank.[65]

- Manufacturing has a poor record of women in positions of leadership. Fewer than 1.3 percent of heavy manufacturing CEOs are women.[66]

- In the oil and gas industry, the number of women in leadership is lower than 1 percent.[67]

This needs to change. If your organization is not making an active attempt at fixing the gender gap at the leadership level, you are missing out on an opportunity. As you can see in figure 6.1, female executives bring strengths of their own to the table (and please note, these are generalizations).

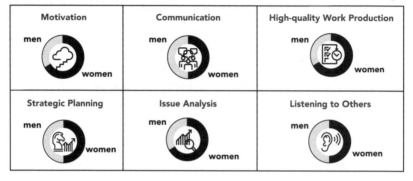

Figure 6.1: Gender differences in the workplace at the executive level[68]

Benefits of gender diversity include the following:

• Once again, a wider talent pool to draw from.

• Better collaboration. While no two people are alike, as figure 6.1 points out, women executives received higher marks in issue analysis, for example—an essential trait for drawing the best from your team.

- Multiple perspectives. You should be hearing from as many of the different axes of diversity as possible. This helps bring about new solutions from different voices.

- Lower turnover. As with diversity in general, employees are more likely to stay at a diverse company. It's an issue that the majority of job candidates feel is important. Women are more likely to stay someplace where they see a future, as evidenced by women in management instead of a sea of male faces.

- A recruiting tool—when women know they will be promoted and are part of the fabric of a company at all levels, they will be more likely to come aboard.

If you are going to ensure that your gender gap closes (if indeed you have one), it's essential that you know some of the issues women face in the workplace today—still:

- Sexual harassment. If you take into account verbal harassment as well as situations of unwanted physical contact, women report numbers as high as nearly 80 percent on experiencing sexual harassment at some point in their careers.[69]

- Pregnancy discrimination.

- Childcare and elder caregiving issues. Women still take on the bulk of these responsibilities.

- Gender pay gaps.

- Racism (in *addition* to gender discrimination).

- The glass ceiling.

- Work-life balance issues.

LGBTQ: EVERYONE IS WELCOME HERE

Companies need to do more than post a rainbow flag on social media in June for Pride month. Roughly 50 percent of LGBTQ workers report having been victims of employee bias at some point in their careers.[70] Your workplace need to be a place that practices respect on every axis.

In addition, currently, over half of US states offer no protection for work discrimination on the basis of gender identity and sexual orientation. The following are some of the issues related to LGBTQ employees:

- Once again, inclusion gives you a wider pool of candidates to draw from.

- Lawsuit risks, public relations risks—today, intolerance is increasingly not tolerated. Negative experiences spread quickly on social media.

- More of today's young people, young employees, and Americans in general support LGBTQ rights than ever before (as high as 72 percent).[71] You will never attract top talent if LGBTQ discrimination is allowed to fester in your workplace. The world is becoming a more open place, and companies need to ensure that all are welcome and feel safe and included.

- Again, people allowed to be their authentic selves bring better performance to the workplace. "Closeted" employees report higher stress levels.[72]

- Diversity policies are important to today's stakeholders, investors, and more.

THE DIVERSITY PIPELINE

Are you still feeling you have a skills gap? That you cannot attract good candidates to fill positions? Still feel like your business or industry is different? You may have a talent shortage! And if you are closing off wells of talent that feed your pipeline—then you may find it becoming increasingly dry. One way to tap the talent pipeline is to ensure you are feeding the diversity pipeline.

It's important to be clear that all of the mission statements, hashtags, and goals about diversity and inclusion mean nothing if you do not enact what you say you are going to do. However, certain industries, for example, might have low percentages of women entering them because of historical discrimination or a lack of encouragement from the industry and society at large. For example, according to the American Association of University Women, girls and young women are still consistently tracked away from going into STEM (science, technology, engineering, and math) in school.[73] Or a company may *want* to find diverse candidates but have problems achieving that.

In short: How can you expand the pools of candidates to a more diverse one in order to fulfill your commitment to a more diverse and inclusive workplace across multiple diverse axes?

- As I seem to shout from the rooftops (all right, I'm not a shouter), there should be an emphasis on *skills*, not degrees.

- Related to that point, beware of socioeconomic bias. By that, again, I mean that degrees sometimes shut out those who can simply not afford the increasingly expensive cost of university or college. Also do not assume that the person with the Harvard degree is automatically a better candidate than the one from a small state school.

- Focus on transferable competencies. As we have explored, there are ways to bring aboard someone from another industry (especially at the entry level) and leverage their skills into a new career. Figure 6.1 illustrates one way in which core competencies from one field are transferable to another.

- Make sure you use gender-neutral language as much as possible, especially when recruiting.

- Do you recruit from HBCUs (Historically Black Colleges and Universities)? Hispanic colleges? What other organizations and institutions can you approach to widen your talent pool?

- How do you signal to the LGBTQ population that you are inclusive? A simple example would be listing preferred pronouns on professional profiles.

- Do you signal to parents that they are welcomed and important to your organization? Do you offer paid maternity *and* paternity leave?

- Does your healthcare plan allow for domestic partnerships? Gender-affirming treatment?

- Does your culture *show* that your company lives your commitment to diversity (which we will cover more deeply in our culture chapter)? Do you have people from many diversity axes in leadership positions?

- If you have diverse employees, then are you ensuring that their referrals are being seriously considered?[74]

- Offer internships to diverse populations.

- Ensure that leadership has had diversity and inclusion training.

- If your company uses recruiters, be aware of their potential biases.[75]

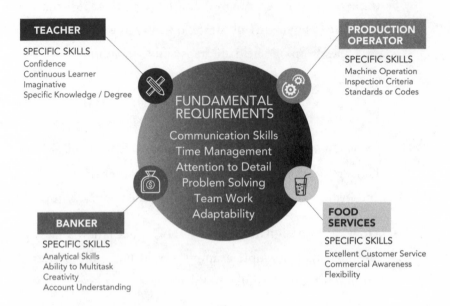

Figure 6.2: Leverage existing skills and transfer competencies

WHO IS BEING HEARD?

Diversity is not a "soup." You cannot just toss a bunch of diverse people into a pot and assume that you are now a diverse organization—or that your diversity is working. Just because you have a diverse group of people doesn't mean that you get good answers or good participation. What you need are openness and sharing.

For diversity to work to the benefit of the company, it must be much more than lip service. I'm going to give an example. A company may bring a recent college grad onto a team. But is that younger voice being heard? Is their opinion welcomed? Or are they just taking up a seat at the table? You might hear from older employees that that new student hasn't learned enough to offer relevance to the issue. They would be wrong.

One example from the medical profession found that younger doctors had lower mortality rates than older doctors! They have learned new techniques and medical technologies the older doctors may be unaware of.[76]

At IPC, we have a university student on our board of directors. We added one because we wanted to know what students were thinking. As we are seeking to promote the global electronics industry, we're trying to get more students and young people engaged in the industry. So we added this position on our board, but it isn't simply to be able to say we have a diverse board. They are a voting member—and we give them a voice.

CULTURAL DIVERSITY

You must value the diversity for it to be effective. This means being aware of cultural differences. I remember my first board meeting when one of our members, who is from China and for whom English is not a native language, was very quiet at a table of strong speakers and personalities and leaders. I made a point of pausing and asking this person, "What are your thoughts?" Those from more reserved countries and cultures are unlikely to burst out, "Hey! Shut up for a second so I can get my point across."

So if you want diversity be effective, if it doesn't happen naturally, you have to be able to help it come out.

Is your company being culturally sensitive?

- Does your company offer a space for those who wish to pray during the day, whatever their faith (such as Muslims who wish to complete their Islamic daily prayers)?

- When you have lunch events, is there are always a vegetarian choice? Better yet, when colleagues are fasting during the month of Ramadan, can you forgo all meetings that occur over food or meals?

- If your company does business with other countries around the globe, are your employees sensitive to their communication styles and other differences that may impact the relationship? These can include negotiation styles, foods, body language, and even handshakes.

- Are posters bilingual? Better yet, illustrations on factory floors or those regarding safety can help bridge some language gaps.

- Schedules: Do you allow PTO and flexible schedules around holidays across all faiths and beliefs? Be careful about not booking meetings and important corporate events on days that conflict with various religious observances.

- Work-life balance and family. Different cultures view time spent with coworkers, or home life balance in different ways. For example, do you only ever offer socialization opportunities at happy hours? Is there an unconscious bias against those who take paternity leave or who make home a strong priority or who do not consume alcohol?

- Be aware of unconscious bias or microaggressions. Cultural sensitivity workshops can help people understand how their behaviors or words may be perceived. There was a time in our caveman past when men routinely called their "secretaries" "sweetie" or otherwise behaved in chauvinistic ways. Sometimes we need to bring people kicking and screaming into this century and decade (and if they are unwilling to learn or try to change, then it may be time to part ways, which we will discuss in more detail in the next chapter on culture).

- Be aware of nuances between cultures. The people of some cultures may not offer input unless called upon. Some cultures emphasize *not* delivering negative news and framing everything in the most positive light. Being as aware of other cultures' subtle and unspoken differences as well as overt ones can help to make your workplace a more open and welcoming environment.

I also want to point out this is not a US book—workforce issues span the globe. In Europe, I have noticed more acceptance of differences. Asia is a more homogenous place. But US-based companies must be very careful to understand their global partners. Let me give you an example.

Years ago, the globe became more aware of the issue of child labor. There were countless "sweatshop" scandals. Many companies cracked down on their supply chains and instituted changes to try to end such practices in their factories. I am not naive; I know it is still a problem in some places.

More recently, though, new scandals erupted over the working conditions at some electronics factories in Asia where very long workweeks, as high as seventy-five to eighty hours, were the norm. In response to an outcry over this, some factories implemented a forty-hour workweek. To our Western thinking, this should have made for a much happier workforce.

This was not the case.

In fact, factories that instituted the shorter workweek and shifts found they were losing huge numbers of employees to factories that offered longer workdays and hours as well as overtime. For many young people in the rapidly evolving global giant China, they're not just making money for themselves; they're sending money home. They demonstrate a culture of work over leisure.

Now consider one more thing: there are many people in the United States who work two (or three) jobs. I have not seen any call for them to be limited in their desire to provide for their families or to curb their work ethic. We need to be conscious of how we are framing our views of other places—our lens can be culturally insensitive.

WHAT DOES ALL THIS DIVERSITY, INCLUSION, AND SENSITIVITY GET YOU?

All of the issues discussed in this chapter bring you more cohesive, creative, innovative teams.

At every interview I do, I ask the candidate, "What is your passion?"

The answers never cease to surprise and delight me. They are as varied as people themselves. When I ask the question, I don't actually want to hear, "I am passionate about work." Instead, I am more interested in what fires that person up.

To one person, it might be golf, cycling, traveling, spending time with their family, gardening, rock climbing, teaching Sunday School, reading, playing baseball, or something as obscure as studying the life cycle of the luna moth. Whatever it is, I want to hear about it. I want to see that person's eyes light up. Because if a person can feel passionate about one thing, they can be passionate about the challenges and rewards of working with me at my organization. If they have chosen this career path, and they're a person of passion, they'll find something in the work that they can get passionate about, and you'll get better quality work from them—and a more loyal, more content, happier person.

Passion is a kind of diversity that I want as well—I have not found it necessary to have people lacking passion. But the way most of us arrive at our passion is by being our authentic selves. Authenticity allows us to engage with each other from a position of our strengths.

When a person has to hide a very central part of them, they are not giving their whole self. If an LGBTQ person is not free to discuss their partner or spouse, then every time their colleagues are exchanging "water cooler talk" about their home life, they are excluded or must self-censor.

If an Orthodox Jewish person doesn't feel free to wear his yarmulke at work, an essential part of their lives is missing. If a Muslim cannot pray … same thing. I sincerely believe the days of never mentioning your religion or culture in the workplace are going the way of the dodo. We need to embrace *all*—while at the same time insisting that every colleague is treated with respect.

This can apply to dress, to other outward elements. A woman in hijab. A person with tattoos. Every kind of hairstyle, braids, dreadlocks, and bald included. None of those things have anything to do with whether a person is good at their job. In fact, they will be *better* at their job if they are being themselves.

One more lesson before we move on. I used to joke—I'm talking twenty-five years ago, that the *one* prejudice I had was against "stupid people." What can I say? I was young.

I mentioned this to a colleague when I was frustrated about a project. He said, "John, let's go for a walk."

We decided to go for a walk around the around the block—a very large block, I will add, and he said, "Let me tell you something. There are different kinds of intelligence. Your book learning is not the only intelligence. You might have a streetwise kid who's been homeless, had many hard knocks, and is trying to better himself or herself. If I dropped you into their situation, you wouldn't last a week. That kid can teach you something. In fact, everyone you meet can teach you something."

I took that to heart.

GOOD FOR BUSINESS

The other thing you "get" in return for diversity and inclusion is a better bottom line (because, after all, this is business).

We have a term these days called ESG, which stands for Environmental, Social, and (Corporate) Governance. They used to call these concepts social responsibility.

So what does ESG mean today?

Well, we are all concerned with sustainability. How are we impacting this planet we call home? This includes pollution, waste, and our carbon footprints. We all want clean water, breathable air, and fewer waste products and toxic chemicals.

But social aspects are concerned with the very things this chapter discussed—things like respect, inclusion, diversity (across multiple axes). Governance on ethical and transparent corporate leadership.

These are more than simply nice ideals. Today's investment companies and firms are demanding certain types of reporting from public companies, and it's spreading like wildfire.

In this era of social media, bad experiences, cultural insensitivity, and other negatives can be blasted across Twitter at the speed of light. In terms of ESG, diversity and inclusion comprise *sound business policy*.

It is also the right thing to do.

⊶ KEY CONCEPTS ————————————————

Most of the elements of diversity and inclusion impact your corporate culture. If your corporate culture does not demonstrate that it promotes women, for example, then you are unlikely to attract the best cross-sections of candidates. Thus, diversity and inclusion impact your hiring habits and recruitment too.

We've separated the culture chapter from the diversity and inclusion chapter, but they are intrinsically intertwined.

- Diversity includes many axes, from age, race, religion, ethnicity, gender identity, and sexual orientation to education, veteran status, and disability.

- Diversity leads to better decision making.

- Companies are increasingly making "diversity pledges," and prominent CEOs tout diversity as a path forward to innovation.

- Diversity and inclusion mean nothing without action. You must do more than simply share a rainbow during Pride month.

- Different age cohorts are seeking different things in the workplace.

- Gender inequality is bad for business.

- When people are able to be their full, authentic selves at work and are accepted, they deliver better performances.

- If your company lags in diversity, you need to examine your diversity pipeline. It is not enough to say, "We're not getting diverse candidates." You need to figure out *why* that is and remedy it.

- Beware of unconscious bias in your recruiters.

- Diverse and inclusive companies have better financial outcomes. Increasingly, investors and stakeholders insist on strong diversity.

- Cultural diversity is policy in action—does your company show its commitment to cultural diversity (such as recognizing diverse religious holidays and offering PTO to recognize them)?

- You will never attract top talent without a commitment to diversity and inclusion. Today's employees demand it.

ACME AND NEW CO.: TWO DIFFERENT APPROACHES TO DIVERSITY AND INCLUSION

⊗ ACME AND THE WAY IT'S ALWAYS BEEN

Acme has had the same management team since it was founded. The CEO and his entire board and his C-suite all look alike, are approximately the same age, went to similar Ivy League schools, and are all white. The CEO has asked human resources to work on remedying this in their new hires, but HR complains they never get diverse applicants—and men outnumber female applicants by a ratio of seven to one. There is not a single woman in the C-suite.

Acme has always recruited from the same sources: several well-known universities, including those attended by members of the C-suite. Meanwhile, in the next town, there is an exceptional HBCU—and no one from the company has ever paid it a visit, even though it has an engineering program that would make an ideal partner to find candidates. In addition, Acme has had the same executive search firm for ten years.

In an effort to modernize their benefits package and expand their recruitment efforts, the board approves a new benefits administrator. They add domestic partnership benefits and paternity leave and create a mission statement proclaiming acceptance, regardless of sexual orientation, religion, race, ethnicity, or gender identity. However, the only religious holidays Acme continues to offer are Christmas Eve/Christmas Day and Good Friday/Easter. There are no gender-neutral bathrooms anywhere in the building.

The human resources department makes an effort to recruit more women. However, maternity leave is only four weeks paid, and there is no policy regarding short leaves for caregiving beyond the federally mandated Family and Medical Leave Act. In addition, there is no lounge or facility for breastfeeding mothers to pump on their breaks, and there are no flex-time or job-sharing options.

Acme encourages informal networking on the last Friday of the month. This is almost always a lunch or a happy hour. The happy hour is always at the same place—a loud bar with great wings and seventy-two TV screens with every sporting event possible on. On Fridays, when there is a luncheon paid for by the company, the catering is nearly always from a pork barbecue joint.

Though each employee on the factory floor is afforded two twenty-minute breaks a day, the time is dictated by the manager. No accommodations are made for Muslims who wish to time their breaks for daily prayer. If they do pray, they must do so in a converted storage closet.

Though 40 percent of the workforce in one particular plant is Spanish-speaking, there are no bilingual posters or signs anywhere.

✅ NEW CO. AND A NEW WAY

New Co.'s C-suite is representative of their diversity and mission statements. Women form nearly half of the C-suite and 52 percent of management. People of color are also well represented as well as several older people, along with millennials. A recent job fair at an HBCU yielded fifteen new hires across a number of sectors. Human resources works with three different executive search firms, including one with a Latina business owner who specializes in recruiting bilingual executives. Names and identifiers are removed from résumés when first considered to eliminate unconscious bias.

Today, a group of eight new hires is being given an orientation, including a tour of the facilities.

A walk across the factory floor reveals signage in Spanish and English. However, the signs are also clearly illustrated, helping to bridge any language gaps. The group is shown New Co.'s meditation room as well as its subsidized cafeteria, which offers vegetarian, gluten-free, halal, and kosher options.

New Co. offers ten PTO days a year as well as eleven holidays that reflect holy days of a number of faiths. In addition, employees are paid for two "volunteer" days a year. The new hires note that a variety of natural hair styles, tattoos, and personal styles are visible. In addition, grab rails in the hallway are at a height appropriate for those with disabilities, and ramps are located throughout the building, along with braille signage on the elevators and other locations.

An online directory of employees lists preferred pronouns, and this quarter, employees can choose to use their paid volunteer day to do a mentorship with LGBTQ teens, something the company sponsors every June for Pride, or to do a beach cleanup, or to spend the day with the charity of their choice.

In addition, they are told that there will be a supplier diversity fair on Friday in an effort to meet new suppliers that reflect a commitment to using more minority-owned businesses in the supply chain.

When the new hires go over their healthcare and benefits packages, they learn that the company offers adoption help for same- and opposite-sex couples, fertility treatments, and gender-affirming healthcare. Mental health services are offered at no cost or copay to employees, and there is a monthly brown bag topic lunch with a psychologist on a variety of topics from stress and burnout to conflict resolution.

CHAPTER SEVEN

WHAT'S YOUR COMPANY CULTURE?

Attracting and Retaining Talent by the Culture You Cultivate

Hire great people and give them freedom to be awesome.
—ANDREW MASON, FOUNDER, GROUPON

A positive corporate culture doesn't happen by accident. Thoughtful ideas and values, along with hiring practices, compensation, "perks," atmosphere, and more come together to create an environment where people want to work (or you screw up—and they *don't*). *Fortune* conducted a Great Place to Work survey, and in 2022, the top company ranked was Cisco, an information technology corporation. According to *Fortune*, the results, based on approximately 870,000 employee surveys, analyze these following areas that employees say are important to them and their work culture:[77]

- High levels of trust

- Respect

- Credibility

- Fairness

- Pride

- Camaraderie

Some of the reasons those surveyed ranked Cisco so highly included things like fairness, the ability to take time off if needed (flexibility), and a sense of safety and acceptance, regardless of race or sexual orientation.[78] Cisco credits seeking employees with a high emotional quotient or EQ who are nurturing, providing their employees with the tools necessary to succeed, giving employees time off to make a difference through volunteering, and emphasizing diversity and inclusion as some of their focuses in developing a workplace of the future.[79]

According to Inc., corporate culture can be defined as:

The shared values, attitudes, standards, and beliefs that characterize members of an organization and define its nature. Corporate culture is rooted in an organization's goals, strategies, structure, and approaches to labor, customers, investors, and the greater community. As such, it is an essential component in any business's ultimate success or failure.[80]

You may recall from chapter one that acquisition and retention are two circles of a Venn diagram with overlap. Culture is one of the key areas that has a critical role in each. You cannot attract the best people if your corporate culture is a negative one, and you cannot retain the best people in a troubled culture either. Culture includes diversity, pathways, onboarding, and more—all the areas that contribute to what it is like to come aboard your company and stay there. Part of culture, for example, is knowing there is a path for growth versus feeling as though your position and the company are stagnant. Part of it is a company's ethics. Part of it is whether you can wear jeans on Fridays. Part of it is who is promoted or given a spot at the boardroom table. It all works together to create your company culture.

> **Culture includes diversity, pathways, onboarding, and more—all the areas that contribute to what it is like to come aboard your company and stay there.**

Corporate culture varies by country and industry. It also shape shifts at times. For example, thirty years ago, very few companies or employees were talking about ESG (Environment, Social, and Governance). Something even as simple and basic as corporate dress code has changed over the years. Goldman Sachs released the following memo in 2019:

> *Given … the changing nature of workplaces … in favor of a more casual environment, we believe this is the right time to move to a firmwide flexible dress code. Please dress in a manner that is consistent with your clients' expectations. We trust you will consistently exercise good judgment in this regard. All of us know what is and is not appropriate for the workplace.*[81]

The three-piece suit is dead.

OLD TITLE AND PRIOR SKILLS	CURRENT TITLE AND CURRENT SKILLS
SECRETARY • Shorthand • Live note taking • Fast/Accurate typing • Organizing and filing skills	**ADMINISTRATIVE ASSISTANT** • Strategic planning • MS Office skills • Technological abilities • Professional communication
TEACHER • Instruction skills • Leadership skills • Strong people skills • Organizational skills • Verbal & handwriting skills	**TEACHER** • All the 'prior' skills • Classroom management software and systems • Electronic presentations • Virtual meetings • Web navigation • MS Office software
GRAPHIC DESIGNER • Fine art skills • Copy/cutting • Waxing & pasting skills • Ink drawing skills	**GRAPHIC DESIGNER** • Advanced Adobe skills • Fine art skills • Pre-press print production • Strong Office skills • Modeling/rendering
MARKETER • Print ad development • Mail marketing • Collateral development • People skills • Sales team coordination	**DIGITAL MARKETER** • Social media outreach • Digital media development • Communication skills • SEO and web-related skills

Table 7.1: Examples of differences between historical roles and expectations of similar roles today

The global COVID-19 pandemic was another game changer for most companies—it fundamentally altered corporate culture rapidly as people had to adjust to working from home or working remotely. However, it was more than simply changing the location of work from the corporate office to the kitchen table. Remote work allowed flexibility, contributing to work-life balance; it eliminated onerous commutes (some employees in places like LA and New York City "gained" close to three hours in their day); it focused employees and teams on what they could get done more than where that work was performed. Most found that productivity was not affected. Like letting a genie out of a bottle, it is unlikely that this change will ever completely go back to how it was.

In chapter two, we discussed the "way, way back" time machine. Culture is influenced not only by a company's leadership and employees but also by social changes. It reflects the times in which we live. Some big changes since the post-WWII boom include the following:

- Greater participation of women in the workplace, including management. According to the Bureau of Labor Statistics, 40 percent of managers in the US workforce, for instance, are now women.[82]

- More diversity, more inclusion. (Though there is still work to do. For example, today, fewer than 1 percent of CEOs in the Fortune 500 are African American.[83])

- Hierarchical structure has morphed in some companies to a more team-oriented structure.

- Sexual harassment was not even *introduced* into the lexicon until 1975.[84]

- US office culture went from cubicles to open spaces—to now, often, remote.

- Technology has changed every single aspect of today's workplace culture.

Culture cannot be "imposed." It generally doesn't spring up overnight but instead over years. In companies with positive culture, this can be through vision and leadership. In companies with negative culture, it can be through stagnation, the "way it's always been," and poor leadership. There's no magic wand to change a culture overnight—but culture can be shaped and changed by a company committed to change and making things better (which we will discuss toward the end of the chapter).

> **There's no magic wand to change a culture overnight—but culture can be shaped and changed by a company committed to change and making things better.**

According to Dr. Edgar Schein, a professor emeritus at MIT's Sloane School of Management:

> In a mature company run by promoted general managers, as opposed to entrepreneurs or founders, the culture will reflect the past history of founders and leaders and will limit what kind of leadership is possible. If a new leader such as Carly Fiorina comes into a company like Hewlett-Packard with a long history and strong culture, there will be conflict between what the new leader tries to impose and what the culture will allow. The leader will win in such conflict only by firing large numbers of the carriers of the old culture, as turnaround managers usually do. The new leader can then start [fresh] by imposing new values and behavior patterns.

But this is not a new culture until it succeeds for a number of years and becomes internalized by the employees. So you can talk about *destroying* an old culture, but you cannot create or *impose* a new culture, only new values and behavior patterns.[85]

WHAT DO EMPLOYEES WANT?

Employees cite a variety of "wants" they would like to see reflected in the companies they work for. They want to feel valued; they want to feel as if their jobs have purpose. Some of the things they are seeking include work-life balance, fair compensation, diversity and inclusion, flexibility (including hybrid and work-from-home options), and well-being measures. In fact, 68 percent of senior human resources professionals cited employee well-being and mental health as being very important.[86]

Well-being measures include a commitment to employees' mental health as well as a holistic view of employees.[87] The pandemic laid bare some of the stresses of today's modern workers. Many parents had to scramble to find childcare in the pandemic so that they could work uninterrupted from their home offices or kitchen tables. Others who could not work remotely went to work with additional fears about their own health and that of their families. Rents and home prices in the United States have outpaced cost-of-living raises. The United States has some of the most stressed workers in the world.[88] Much of it is related to the familiar refrain of "work-life balance." Technology allowed us to Zoom into meetings—but technology and being a text away from work, regardless of time or time zone, often blur the lines between professional and personal lives.

In addition to showing that in some positions and industries, remote work does not lead to less productivity, the global pandemic altered the values of today's modern employees. This was not merely an American phenomenon. For instance, in Australia, a survey of five hundred people revealed that 65 percent say that what they value most about their jobs has changed since the pandemic.[89]

At IPC, we went remote years ago, as I have mentioned elsewhere in the book. This was a cultural shift—and since it was before this was as common as it is now, it involved figuring it out without a model for how to do so. I think it's going to be increasingly difficult to attract top talent if flexibility and more options for remote or hybrid work are not part of your organization (again, for some positions).

As we saw in our diversity and inclusion chapter, not everyone seeks the same thing in jobs and corporate culture. A great example is a recent Glassdoor survey. Among millennials, 65 percent ranked diversity over *salary*; that number dropped to 52 percent among those over forty-five. This result was repeated with similar percentages in the United Kingdom.[90]

HarperCollins union employees and supporters, in July of 2022, went on a one-day strike to call attention to their desires for the workplace. Most publishing professionals work in New York City (remote and hybrid work may be changing that), a very expensive place to live in, work in, and commute to. The starting salaries for associate editors fall at $45,000 and below. The employees went on strike for better pay—but also better family leave benefits as well as a greater commitment from HarperCollins to diversity.[91]

However, despite any differences in employee engagement factors, passion and purpose motivate people. A positive corporate culture attracts top talent, it delivers better performances, and it improves your brand (see the Happy Marriott story later in the chapter).

WHAT DO YOU STAND FOR?

There's an apocryphal quote misattributed to Alexander Hamilton that nonetheless states: "Those who stand for nothing will fall for anything." Most people need to believe in something, to have those feelings of passion and purpose that are so essential to bringing out the best in us all. Employees want to see their values reflected where they work. Mission statements reflect those values of your company. However, they are only as good as the implementation.

Let's look at the mission statements of some top companies:

- Patagonia: We're in business to save our home planet.[92]

- IKEA: To offer a wide range of well-designed, functional home furnishing products at prices so low that as many people as possible will be able to afford them.[93] (Note, there will also be a lot of nuts and bolts.)

- TED: Spread ideas.[94]

Mission statements describe a company in the "now." Those missions may change over time as a company grows or significantly changes, the brand expands or alters, or a company's customers or audience changes. For example, if your company started out making computer monitors but now makes a huge range of electronics products and technology, the mission statement you started with may no longer apply. In other words, a mission statement is a reflection of who that company is and what its mission is at that moment in time.

There are also *vision* statements. Think of a vision statement as "the big idea" or "the big purpose." A vision statement is a road map of where the company wants to go versus a snapshot in time. It is a reflection of the future and what the company aspires to. Here are a couple of examples:

- Pepsi: "Our vision is put into action through programs and a focus on environmental stewardship, activities to benefit society, and a commitment to build shareholder value by making PepsiCo a truly sustainable company. At PepsiCo, we're committed to achieving business and financial success while leaving a positive imprint on society—delivering what we call Performance with Purpose."[95]

- Amazon: "Our vision is to be earth's most customer centric company; to build a place where people can come to find and discover anything they might want to buy online."[96]

To revisit Ikea, their *vision* statement is: To create a better everyday life for the many people.[97]

However, neither mission nor vision statements are meaningful without corporate buy-in to those values. They cannot be empty words. For example, Patagonia donates at least 1 percent of its sales to many different environmental groups around the world.[98] And their founder gave the company to an organization dedicated to fighting climate change.[99]

Let's look at two companies where their visions, missions, and purposes help drive their success.

SONY KANDO

Companies are increasingly expanding their vision—in more ways than one. While five-year plans are important, some companies create fifty- and hundred-year plans. The idea is that the succession and the company go on long after the founders depart. Sony famously had a fifty-year vision plan from the outset. It also prides itself on its culture.

To that end, Sony has a term: "Kando." Their CEO at the time it was introduced, Kazuo Hirai, defined it: "Kando translates to mean emotional involvement. The power to stimulate an emotional response. The power to make people say, 'Wow.' All Sony products must be inspired by a spirit of Kando."[100]

Part of Sony's culture is thus about the power of connecting emotionally. In fact, they bring influencers, employees, and others to Kando events where photography is explored but through the lens, if you will, of emotional connection. Other elements of Sony's stated cultural goals include the following:[101]

- Sony's "purpose" is "to fill the world with emotion, through the power of creativity and technology.

- Its stated values include dreams and curiosity, diversity, integrity and sincerity, and sustainability.

- Its entertainment sector's principles include the highest standards; top talent; transparency, openness, and inclusion; collaboration and integration; focus on the consumer; and "big thinking."

All of these elements work together to create Sony's culture (as well as their brand).

HAPPY MARRIOTT

A colleague once told me a story about the Marriott hotel chain. He was checking into a property, and during every encounter he had with employees, they went "above and beyond"—with a smile! But beyond that, they possessed an energy that most companies would be envious of. Employees seemed genuinely happy (in fact, if you Google "Happy Marriott," you will see that Marriott prides itself on happy employees and a commitment to employee well-being). As I said at the outset of this chapter, such a culture does not happen by accident. Marriott seeks out happy and enthusiastic people to become their employees (it is difficult to take a miserable, unhappy person and transform them into a happy one; if it were easy, we would all do so in both our personal and professional lives). So if Marriott intentionally cultivates a happy workplace, how is that achieved and reflected through its culture and values?

For starters, Marriott's motto *since its inception* is: "Take care of your employees, they'll take care of your customers and the customers will keep coming back again and again."[102]

While intentional leadership is important, Marriott places its greater weight on its people—its employees. This is reflected in its five core values:[103]

1. Put people first.

2. Pursue excellence.

3. Embrace change.

4. Act with integrity.

5. Serve our world.

Marriott's leadership believes that one of the most important things people who work there want is "purpose in their lives."[104] It can seem difficult to measure culture, purpose, and employee satisfaction—some of these concepts may sound almost mystical. However, Marriott commissioned a longitudinal study that directly correlated employee engagement to improved hotel financial performance.[105]

PERKS VERSUS PASSION AND PURPOSE

When I came aboard IPC, I didn't come in like the proverbial bull in a china shop. I needed to make changes—after all, that was why I was brought aboard. But I also needed to *listen* and *observe*.

Now I am not a coffee drinker (I know, shocking!). At some point, providing coffee stations and free coffee was mentioned as something the employees wanted. Done. That's sort of a no-brainer. It does not really affect our bottom line, and it is a gesture of goodwill that employees (all those caffeine drinkers) appreciate. However, don't confuse perks with passion and purpose.

In the heady heyday of Silicon Valley start-ups, unbelievable perks became part of the allure of certain companies. I can recall news segments or articles touting stories of juice bars, beer served on Fridays, basketball and handball courts, and assorted other office extras. I don't consider benefits like healthcare and dental care as "perks." They are benefits (discussed next) that I think are extremely important to offer employees. Perks can be things like sleeping pods, free dry cleaning, discounts on products the company makes, massage therapists on site, gyms on site, and yes, company-sponsored happy hours, fancy lunchrooms, and off-site events.

However fun or attractive to some people these "perks" might be, however, they are not the same as employees sharing a collaborative vision, a core culture that makes them passionate, fulfilled, and challenged at their jobs. Perks may be pieces of your corporate culture, but they are not reasons that people will come aboard and stay. This leads us to a discussion of benefits.

BENEFITS: DOES YOUR BENEFITS PACKAGE REFLECT YOUR CULTURE?

Benefits are part of an employee compensation package. They are also a reflection of your culture because they demonstrate what it is your company values. Not what you *say* you value, but in fact, what you *show* that you value.

If you don't *show* it, your employees will see through you that your commitment is not what you say it is. Here are some examples that show a disconnect between stated values and actual values:

- A company that claims to value employee well-being but only allows two personal days a year.

- A company that claims to want to build a climate of trust but forces employees to pass through metal detectors as a theft deterrent.

- A company that claims to value employee health but limits bathroom breaks, or worse, times them via RFID devices.

- A company that claims to value work-life balance but offers no flextime for positions where that would not be an issue. This one can apply to trust as well.

- A company that says it values its employees' families but offers no paid maternity or paternity leave.

Now let's look at examples that demonstrate companies whose benefits reflect their commitment to their employees.

- A company that values employee "well-being" and provides free telehealth and mental healthcare.

- A company that says it wants to grow its employees and provides free tuition. (Starbucks, for example, offers 100 percent free tuition at an online university for first-time bachelor's degree candidates.)[106]

- A company that says it values work-life balance and provides generous or unlimited vacation days or personal days.

- A company that says it values family life and provides adoption assistance for its employees.

When I came aboard IPC, and it was time to revisit our benefits package and its cost, I inquired about the difference in cost to the company between a health plan with moderate levels of copays and one that had no copays for routine care. While there was a difference, it was not out of the question in our budget. I approved the better healthcare plan—with the company paying the cost difference. I viewed it as what *I* would want. Not only did I feel that it was the right thing to do, but it also sent a powerful message to our employees. They are valued, and we care about their health and well-being—as well as the health and well-being of their families.

LEADERSHIP

Your company leadership is a reflection of your culture. MIT conducted a study that looked at different aspects of corporate culture. In the area of leadership, employees cited the following as important: supportive leaders and leaders living core values.[107] In that same survey, toxic managers and unethical behavior are two types of negative leadership that impact how employees feel about the corporate culture where they work.[108]

Leadership affects company culture by:

- Setting rules and policies (that ideally will reflect the company's positive values).

- Who they hire. Who they retain. (This is reflected in diversity and inclusion, as well as what is tolerated behavior—we will address this shortly in the bad apples section.)

- How they react to crises and tough times.[109]

- How they treat subordinates and teams.[110]

- What is praised and rewarded.[111]

Positive leadership is reflected in a positive workplace, in positive morale, in employee retention, in a talent pipeline created through having a place where people outside the company desire to work. Negative leadership can be a drag on the entire workplace. Poor leadership traits include:

- Lack of integrity

- Inflexibility ("my way or the highway" thinking)

- Poor communication style (people are not mind-readers)

- Fear-based or intimidation-style leadership

- Lack of transparency

- People who think they know everything

- Those who take sole credit for team projects

- Micromanagement

Great leaders have a vision that they can communicate clearly; they are humble (they don't know everything—and are OK with that and surround themselves with smart people); they uplift people; they realize they may report to a board—but they *answer* to their employees; they realize those employees are their company's most valuable assets; they are respectful to all; and they lead by *example*.

POSITIVE LEADERSHIP EXAMPLES

Positive leadership requires … *leaders*. True leadership doesn't necessarily have to do with a name on a corner office or C-suite door. Natural leaders are found in every level of a company. A promotion or a salary bump does not automatically bestow positive leadership traits (which points back to culture evolving by who is promoted and who is hired). People lead—and companies take the lead. Here are a couple of examples of companies that demonstrated real leadership in trying times:

- After 9/11, many airlines began laying off employees as fears of flying decimated the industry. Southwest Airlines' CEO, however, believed the company had created an airline with solid business principles. Rather than laying off employees, he kept them all on *and* started a profit-sharing plan for them.[112]

- Former Costco CEO Jim Sinegal made efforts to personally visit all his locations and wore a basic name tag reading "Jim." At the time, he was collecting a salary of $350,000—not an outrageous compensation package compared to many a CEO at the time.[113] He also famously told his successor if he raised the price of the hot dog and soda combo above $1.50, he would [insert expletive]-ing kill him![114]

Steve Jobs was a visionary—and his leadership took Apple from a struggling company to one ubiquitous in American culture through its iPhone. Bill and Melinda Gates took the lead with their foundation in weaving philanthropic purpose with brand and beliefs. Leaders have taken companies through economic downturns, crises, massive expansion, and day-to-day commitments to making a difference and building a brand. Leaders ... lead.

ETHICS AND INTEGRITY

Whole books are written on ethics and integrity alone.

I will be completely truthful. In my career, I would only ever resign from a position for one of two reasons. The first would be finding that I am unable to work with the person I reported to. I generally can get along with anyone, so it would not be something I take lightly, and I would only leave after giving maximum effort to trying to forge a relationship. The second would have to do with ethics or integrity. I live my life by a set of principles, and it is simply not worth it to me to work for a company or a person who did not reflect a similar degree of integrity.

While many people use the terms *ethics* and *integrity* interchangeably, in actuality, there is a difference between the two. Ethics is a set of principles. They are situational, however. For example, you might say it is ethical to *never* lie. But there could be a case where a white lie might be ethical (think of telling a child that they will "always" be safe—we cannot actually promise that, but for a six-year-old, that is a statement that is appropriate for now). Integrity is living one's life by your (or a company's) principles at all times—even when it's inconvenient—such as not covering up something negative and dealing with it head on. One is what you espouse; the other is how you live and who you are. A company can impose ethics ("We will not discriminate on the basis of …"). But they cannot impose integrity. In other words, a person in authority may not believe those principles—or act that way all the time.

We can define business ethics as the standards and moral guidelines for how a business conducts itself in the marketplace and with both internal and external stakeholders. Integrity, on the other hand, according to *Merriam-Webster*, is a "firm adherence to a code of especially moral or artistic values" and "incorruptibility."[115] Integrity encompasses your core values.

Sometimes a company fails due to its lack of ethical leadership—and that fall can be spectacularly precipitous. Think of Enron, the fall of the Lehman Brothers, Dennis Kozlowski at Tyco, and Turing Pharmaceuticals' "Pharma Bro," CEO Martin Shkreli. In today's "viral" social media world, ethics and integrity not only are the right things to do—but they also make good business

An ethical culture does not develop in a vacuum.

sense. Ethical violations can not only cost a company in its bottom line (through fines, decline in value of stocks, and in loss of business) but also in its somewhat intangible brand recognition and value.

However, like a positive workplace culture, an ethical culture does not develop in a vacuum. The following are elements important to ethical workplaces:

- The leadership allows for and admits mistakes. Your corporate culture cannot be ethical in a climate of fear. Being able to approach leadership with problems or mistakes is essential to an ethical culture.

- Define your values—then live by them.

- Ensure that ethical behavior is expected and rewarded. Ethical lapses can occur in intense environments where key performance indicators, quotas, and so on are valued over *how* that is achieved. A win-at-any-cost mentality is a surefire way to lead to ethical lapses.

- If ethical lapses cannot be retrained or corrected, it is time to part ways. Show your team what it is you value.

- "Teach" ethics. At team meetings, have managers and leadership explore ethical situations and explore how employees would handle them.

In terms of integrity, I will be frank: it cannot be taught. Someone either has integrity or they don't. It is *not* situational. We will discuss bad apples later, but understand that allowing lapses of integrity is a slippery slope. A seemingly small "theft" or poor behavior that is not addressed merely tells that person that they got away with it—and they can do it again. And it tells the colleagues around them the same.

DIVERSITY AND INCLUSION

In our previous chapter, we explored diversity and inclusion. A majority of today's modern employees generally value inclusion—and studies demonstrate this in a variety of ways.

- Among millennials, 83 percent report high engagement levels when they believe the company they work for is inclusive.[116]

- In terms of the bottom line, 75 percent of companies with diverse and inclusive cultures will meet or exceed their financial goals and expectations.[117]

- A 2019 survey found that 70 percent of respondents would consider switching jobs or looking for a new job if their current company was not committed to diversity.[118]

The world is vast. And it is also small. Consequently, many of us know people and work with people who are very different from us. That could be in terms of race, gender identification, sexuality, religion, politics, and overall belief systems. Part of a corporate culture is ensuring that all of those people feel safe and feel valued and respected. Remember when you were a kid and you were told "If you can't say anything nice, don't say anything at all"? Well, a similar mindset can apply to diversity and inclusion. Your company cannot force an employee to approve or "like" someone else's religious choice, or choice of spouse, or gender identification. However, your company *can* insist that you treat your coworker who is different from you respectfully.

CHANGING CULTURE

One of the trickiest aspects of *Firing Your Hiring Habits* is changing your corporate culture. One of the most difficult things to achieve in a standing organization is to change its culture, as my earlier quote from Edgar Schein alluded to. Changing corporate culture is often done through massive personnel changes because *people are the culture.*

You can't just suddenly put up new signs and think that suddenly you are a happy, friendly place when the company is full of cubicle curmudgeons. You cannot claim all employees will be respected if you have managers going ballistic all the time. You cannot say you are committed to ethics when, if an employee reports a serious violation, nothing actually happens. You cannot espouse wanting to modernize and move forward in this century if the party line is "But we've always done it this way ..."

Culture is to recruiting as product is to marketing.
—HUBSPOT'S CULTURE CODE

Here are some things to consider if you desire to change your corporate culture.

LOOK FOR OPPORTUNITIES

First, you will likely want to gradually spread your new culture (a bit like planting seeds) or gradually replace people to create the desired culture.

Every time I change somebody, I'm looking for someone *better*. Even if I loved the employee who is leaving for another company, it's an opportunity for *me*. Essentially, when I hired that person, they were the best person I could find. (And more often than not, I've been right about that.) While I may be disappointed to see someone leave, I am usually rather excited about it. Now that they're leaving, I know what worked about that person—and am aware of new traits or qualities or experiences I might be seeking in the new hire to replace them.

I am a firm believer that positive attracts positive. I look at the positives of the person who is leaving, and I build on that. Here's a fun personal story. One of my executives decided to leave IPC to take a job working with government. He called me just before we were supposed to go to Paris for a conference and meetings. He had already given us a month's notice. He asked me if I still wanted him to go to Paris.

"You still work for us, don't you?"

He laughed and said yes.

Then I explained, "I am very happy about your new job. It's a terrific fit for you. And now I get to find your replacement. I know what I want—all the boxes you tick. But now I can look for someone even better ... maybe tick a few more boxes."

Of course, I said this in a playful way. But I meant it. There is opportunity when you lose someone. In this guy's case, he was great in moving the organization forward. But his leaving gave me the opportunity to "level up" in that position! Maybe someone else leaves, and you know what you *don't* want next time. And by the way … soon after coming aboard, his replacement got me a meeting with the president of the United States in the White House and a member of the European Union Parliament in Brussels. Leveling up indeed!

LISTEN AND OBSERVE

You cannot change a culture until you know what it is and what's wrong (and right) with it. Negative cultural issues are very often the tip of the iceberg, with much of the danger and potential damage hidden under the surface.

As an example, if the supervisors or managers in a large company are only white men in their fifties and sixties who have been at the company for years, and there have been no promotions of women or minorities or younger staff, the factory floor may run fine—but it certainly will feel like a stifling, stagnant environment for the people working there, especially women or minorities. When people do not see themselves reflected in management, the subconscious message is that the employee best be content staying where they are because they do not "see" themselves in any of the leadership positions.

When I came aboard IPC, I spent time listening and observing. I also don't mean I only spent time listening to managers. I would go out to lunch with cross-functional groups of employees at all levels and listen to their pains and frustrations as well as their joys and successes. We did surveys. I spent time trying to understand the industry and changes within it, as well as challenges. Changes weren't made in a "throw the spaghetti at the wall and see what sticks" way.

When I did spearhead changes (after listening to teams of employees representing all levels of the company), we met with oppo-

FIRE YOUR HIRING HABITS

sition. Change makes some people uncomfortable (others may find it invigorating).

In fact, one of my vice presidents, who had been with the company "forever," and whose father had been with the company before him (so he knew the history of the entire organization), told me,

"When you first came, John, I thought you were going to kill the organization."

But on the "other side" of some of our changes, this person opined, "We're stronger and better than we ever have been."

You must also be aware, like my friend above pointed out, that sometimes, change is painful—but necessary. You don't change for the sake of change or to put your stamp on things. You change for the right reasons.

A good example of that was when I came aboard as CEO, as an early riser, I preferred to have meetings at 9:00 a.m. However, I came to discover that the company had "core hours" (ten o'clock to three o'clock), and flextime was built around that, culminating in a 37.5-hour workweek. After a great deal of thought and study, I moved us to a forty-hour workweek. *However,* I recognized a change like that would face resistance and unhappiness. The solution is to create a win-win environment. Extra personal time as well as days off for employees to perform volunteer work were added simultaneously, which transitioned our change more smoothly.

Some people will be very supportive. Some will resist. They may resist to your face or be confrontational, overtly negative, etc. Or they may be passive-aggressive or be that part of the iceberg that is beneath the surface, resisting in ways that may not be overt. Resistance does not mean you stop reaching for positive change. In a sense, as a company moves forward, as the culture changes, the people who are negative or do not possess the values you are seeking will no longer feel comfortable where they are and very likely may search for new positions that fit them.

FIRE FAST, HIRE SLOW

Early on, this book's proposed title was *Fire Fast, Hire Slow.* I was concerned, however, that the word "fire" would give the wrong idea, as if firing people could be taken lightly. So when it comes to culture, let me explain what I mean.

First, there are non-negotiables. There are lines that cannot be crossed—ever. Determine what those are at your company. For example, if your factory floor manager refers to an ethnic group or members of the LGBTQ community with a derogatory term or makes off-color jokes, there is certainly room to educate this person to make *absolutely clear* that intolerance will not be tolerated. However, if they continue to reject that retraining, they must go. The non-negotiables mean just that.

Another good example would a male member of an older generation who consistently speaks to women in the workplace as if this were still the *Mad Men* generation. Despite correction after correction, his behavior does not change. Sorry, but being from an older generation is not an excuse. Times change, and it is important to change with them. If this person will not learn the decorum of the modern workplace, it is time to part ways—or isolate this person.

In terms of hiring, you may recall that I said that referrals, for example, are a great way to hire. The reason for this is that even if you use the "rule of three" in interviewing, you have a very limited number of hours to get a feel for a potential employee. Not rushing into a hire is always wise advice. There are bullet points on a résumé and various certifications, say, but there are more intangible parts of how a person will fit in your culture—particularly if you are trying to move your culture in a new direction. If the referring employee has more experience (years perhaps) with that new hire, you are minimizing your risk.

CREATIVELY USING LAYOFFS

There are numerous stories of companies that avoided layoffs in creative ways (employees deferring some compensation, employees investing in the company, employees taking a temporary pay cut so no one has to be let go in a recessionary time). Very often, ethics columns and other business discussions revolve around whether layoffs are OK or necessary. I personally have had this question put to me in lectures I have given.

In times when it might be necessary because of a downturn in business to do a layoff, this can actually *help* in your aim to create a more positive culture. This can be the time to zero in on those not fully onboard with your changes, problematic employees, and the like.

Layoffs still must be done with the highest ethics. However, it is an opportunity to make a change in your culture more in keeping with your vision and mission and aspirations in regard to your workplace environment.

BAD APPLES

One of the biggest mistakes a leader can make when it comes to corporate culture is to allow bad apples to remain. Perhaps they commit a "non-negotiable" like fraud, sexual harassment, or discrimination—but bad apples can be more subtle. Trust me, there is plenty of bad behavior to go around. Bad apples might include the following:

- Bullies and "yellers" who rule by fear

- Disagreeable people who cannot seem to get along with anyone in any team situation

- Negative complainers about *everything*

- Those who take advantage of or don't follow the rules—things like taking multi-hour lunches a couple of times a week, those who consistently do not come in on time when their position requires it, those who don't do their fair share of the work (but have plenty of criticism for those who do), those who never take responsibility for mistakes

Bad apples really can poison teams or workplaces. William Felps, a researcher, explored the phenomenon after his wife had a negative experience in the workplace.[119] His wife noticed that when a particular caustic, negative coworker was out for several days due to illness, the entire mood of her department changed. People were less tense and more relaxed, and there was more teamwork, conversation, and camaraderie. Felps discovered that a single bad apple employee really could spoil a workplace.

Ideally, you want to avoid hiring a bad apple in the first place. Here, the advice is "hire slow." Check references carefully; bring the potential hire in more than once for interviews with different people in different situations to see whether their demeanor changes in other circumstances.

What do you do about a bad apple who's already *there*? The best thing to do is to legally, respectfully, but firmly make plans to part ways. Sometimes that can be done during a layoff. Sometimes that may involve isolating them from others in another position where they do not interact with a team (which may prompt them to look for a new job) or, like ripping off a Band-Aid, firing them.

The worst decision would be to keep them, though. By the way, I am not talking about someone who is going through a personal crisis, such as an employee who has recently lost their life partner and is not fully "present" in the workplace and not producing in this situation. Empathy, compassion, and humanity dictate that we need to care about our employees' well-being and to understand that life, death, illness, and more happens. We're all not at 100 percent in the workplace all the time. Instead, I mean people who spread negativity, gossip, complain, and drag down others with them, while at the same time not doing their jobs (they're too busy complaining!).

The most difficult task is when you have a bad apple who is a critical piece of your business solution. Separation can be, as they say, "sweet sorrow," but for your team culture necessary. No one is irreplaceable.

When you keep a bad apple, you must ask yourself: What does it say to my other employees and colleagues that we are all well aware that this person is toxic, but we allow their behavior—and employment—to continue?

RELIGION (YES, YOU REALLY CAN "GO THERE")

In our final chapter, I will discuss this topic more fully, but there has long been a taboo about bringing up any aspect of religion at work. However, there must be some clarification about that.

Part of the reason that religion has been a topic to avoid in the workplace was wanting to ensure that when someone wanted to share their religion, the receiving party did not feel compelled to accept due to the position of the individual sharing. However, in our chapter on diversity and inclusion, we explored that people put forth their best and most passionate work when they can be fully themselves. In the spirit of inclusiveness, being mindful, say, of not having all social events on a Friday (when, for example, an Orthodox Jew could not attend), not making all social events revolve around alcohol (several religions have that as a no-no, including Baha'i and the Church of Jesus Christ of Latter-Day Saints), allowing prayer space for Muslims or others who might wish to observe prayer times during the day, and being careful about scheduling important meetings on holy days of various faiths, is important. But more than that, allowing people to observe their religion at work—as long as it does not offend or demean others—allows their "whole selves" to show up. Studies have shown this results in increased productivity, so there is even a bottom-line benefit![120]

CULTURES ACROSS THE WORLD

It has never been my intent to write a book that only applies to the United States. IPC spans the globe in our scope, as do many companies. Thus, this is a good time to make clear that in a global world, it is wise to be mindful of other cultures—whether that is in dealing with vendors, or with subsidiaries, or factories in countries different from your home base.

For instance, I have emphasized how important I think diversity and inclusion is. However, there are countries (Japan, for example) where there is less ethnic diversity on the basis of its population. Over 98 percent of those living in Japan are Japanese.[121] Diversity hiring goals are simply not applicable on the ethnicity front (though in countries like that, improving the representation of women in management may be).

Those in the C-suite need to recognize that applying Western or US values to operations in other countries is sometimes an apples-to-cake situation—a completely different animal.

Now, to be clear, there are non-negotiables there too. There are wrongs against humanity, child labor, and modern-day slavery that must be rooted out. However, as I explored elsewhere, for example, in some cultures, working sixty hours or more is a norm, and taking away hours to pull them more in line with some Western-norm schedules is not welcomed. Not every culture is seeking a Western definition of "work-life balance," for example.

STEPS TO CHANGE CULTURE

So we've addressed culture and the topics around changing culture. What are the specific steps to creating change and being a change agent, though?

1. **ASSESS YOUR CURRENT CULTURE.** You cannot know what needs changing without knowing where you are starting. As I said in the chapter, when I started as CEO of IPC, I observed, studied, and asked for input from all levels of our company .

2. **PINPOINT WHAT NEEDS TO CHANGE.** It can't be "everything." Specific, measurable goals as far as change should be a part of the process. Accountability should be part of it too.

3. **COMMUNICATE THE CORE VALUES THAT WILL BE PART OF YOUR COMPANY OF THE FUTURE.** Ensure that every single member of your organization knows those values and what they mean

4. **LEAD BY EXAMPLE.** Ensure commitment from leadership at all levels.

5. **COMMIT.** This means not giving up when there are bumps in the road. It also means following the advice in this chapter and knowing what the non-negotiables and "bad apples" are and committing to eliminating those who are not willing to be part of the solution.

6. **KNOW THAT CHANGE IS A PROCESS.** You cannot change a corporate culture overnight.

7. **HIRE AND FIRE INTENTIONALLY.** Both these aspects of corporate human resources should be done with the culture in mind in addition to the needs of the position.

🔑 KEY CONCEPTS

Corporate culture is essential to both acquisition and retention. The following are key points to keep in mind.

- Corporate culture includes values and attitudes, shared goals, and approaches to all aspect of a company both internal and what it projects to the world. It is essential to a business's success or failure.

- Positive culture is intentional. It doesn't happen by accident.

- Employees will consistently rank diversity and inclusion and sharing values with a company over salary in importance.

- A mission statement is a snapshot in time of a company's purpose and meaning.

- A vision statement is a forward-looking plan for where the company wants to be now—and in the future.

- Changing culture takes time and often involves making significant personnel changes along with other adjustments.

- Management must lead by example.

- Ethics and integrity are essential to a company's success.

- Bad apples in a company who are allowed to remain unchecked can poison a corporate culture.

- Corporate culture varies by industry and country or location.

ACME AND NEW CO.: A CONTRAST OF CULTURES

⊗ ACME'S CULTURE WOES

Acme's current culture is embodied by posters on the walls of the factory. These posters have attractive illustrations that tout diversity, inclusion, and commitment to employees. They have a powerful mission statement:

> *At Acme, we are committed to being the world's greatest anvil manufacturer. We want to change the world one anvil at a time, with a focus on exceptional customer service and happy employees.*

Despite the mission statement, no one seems to be particularly happy at Acme. They have a turnover rate 20 percent higher than other same-sized anvil companies in their industry, and despite offering referral bonuses, few in their company ever bring recommendations for potential hires. If the CEO walks around the building, he often hears snippets of grousing and complaining. The CEO orders management—and only management—to do a deep dive into Acme's culture. They do, and they say that everything is fine after months of surveys and studies. However, they decide to devise a new mission statement to see whether that might motivate people. Soon Acme's woes deepen. The board of directors eventually orders the hiring of an outside company to analyze the problems. A team-based examination across all levels of the company occurs. These are their findings:

- Upper-level management is comprised exclusively of white men in their fifties, all of whom have been with the company for two decades or longer.

- The only people of color are on the factory floor.

- There is only a single female manager—and that is of a small department that handles shipping.

- The company provides social events, and they are always at a specific place and always on Fridays, limiting who can attend based on location and the only option being Fridays.

- Five percent of their employees are Jewish. Last year, a mandatory training event was held on Rosh Hoshana.

- Three Muslim employees (all in accounting) have offered to forgo their lunch hours if they can take time for Dhuhr and Asr prayers each day. Their request was denied as being too disruptive. However, the company does allow a Bible study in the lunchroom on Wednesdays—which management says proves their commitment to religious freedom and openness.

- The customer service department has the lowest levels of employee satisfaction and engagement of any department surveyed. Despite being assured that the results are anonymous, none of the surveys are returned with additional comments, despite there being space to do so. When the outside consultants delve further, they discover that the nickname for the manager in that department is Yosemite Sam—because he often launches into tirades. The work environment is of total silence except for the answering of the incoming calls. The turnover rate in that department is double the already-dismal turnover rates. When the consultants ask why Yosemite Sam is allowed his frequent screaming sessions (one infamous, when he swept a desk of all its paperwork onto the floor), he is told that Sam is just two years from retirement, so they are just "riding it out" until then.

- There have been three credible complaints of sexual harassment about the vice president of manufacturing. One lawsuit was settled out of court. He has been sent to sensitivity training. However, his fourth administrative assistant in two years just quit without notice.

- The benefits package for executives is very generous and paid for entirely by the company. The employee benefit package is one of three tiers. In order to choose the highest tier, the biweekly out of pocket would be 9.5 percent of the average employees' wages. The lowest tier has a $9,000 family deductible and a $50 copay for routine office visits. There is no health savings account option.

⊘ NEW CO.'S NEW WAYS

New Co. prides itself on being an open-door company. There is a lounge-type library area where employees can work in a more relaxed atmosphere, and very often, collaboration occurs spontaneously.

The company has a mission statement, a vision statement, and a statement of commitment to diversity and inclusion. These were worked on and written by a committee of people from all areas of the company. Most employees can recite them by heart—and if you ask them, they will tell you that the management and employees take it seriously.

Last year, the director of accounting was told in confidence that one of her managers often made disparaging comments about LGBTQ people, despite having several LGBTQ employees in that department. In general, the department seemed to have less camaraderie than other departments. When asked about his offensive comments, the manager claimed it was all "joking." The manager was sent to a sensitivity program, with one day off site, and several exceptional video modules. Instead of helping to change his objectionable behavior, the manager instead griped about the "stupidity" of sensitivity training to anyone within earshot. After verbal and written warnings, the manager and New Co. parted ways. Recently, the director was passing through the breakroom when she overheard three employees discussing how wonderful it was for a company to actually follow through on their commitments and values statements. The department is now considered one of the best in the company, and the team there often participates in after-work events of a variety of types: a bowling league, a trivia night group at a pub, a lunchtime book club, and a monthly cycling meetup on Saturdays for interested parties.

New Co.'s employees' digital signatures all define pronoun preferences. One new employee recently remarked that the hallways sometimes look "like the United Nations" because so many different types of people and cultures are represented.

New Co. reviews their healthcare plan every year. As usual, the company contributes 90 percent of the cost. There are only two tiers— great and better-than-great. The employees have small deductibles of five dollars. There are low costs for hospital copays, and a health savings account program helps to reduce costs even more.

Finally, New Co. *encourages* both paternity and maternity leaves for parents and offers adoption assistance and assorted other benefits. They provide free mental health therapy and substance abuse counseling for any employee needing it. In addition, it is known throughout the company that working on weekends is frowned upon and that vacations should not only be taken—they should be free of disruptions from the office. Tai chi and meditation classes at lunch hour and company-wide "wellness" days when a free mobile health screening team comes reflect New Co.'s commitment to reducing stress and burnout.

CHAPTER EIGHT

GETTING HELP

Companies Are Not in the Education Business

---

*Education is not the learning of facts, but
the training of the mind to think.*
—ALBERT EINSTEIN

WHAT DO YOU NEED: A DEGREE OR SKILLS?

In martial arts, people start out as a white belt. Depending on the discipline—karate, tae kwon do, etc.—a person can take three or four years or more, depending on how hard they work, their dedication, their instructor, etc. to become a black belt. That black belt represents many, many hours of practice, workouts, discipline, and study. The person will learn various kicks, punches, board-breaking techniques, choreographed forms, and more. They will be bruised, tired, and achy. And finally, it will culminate in a lengthy and intense black belt examination. Then, the *real* learning begins. Wait, what? I earn my black belt, and *then* I start learning? Yes. And that's not all that unusual.

In engineering, someone can go through school—study intensely for four years to become an electrical engineer, chemical engineer, biotechnology engineer, and so on. They will graduate. Get a job. And they will now need to be educated or trained because without practical skills and competencies, they simply are a "baby" in the world of engineering with much to learn.

I have a few letters after my name, including EdD. For my doctorate, I have studied much of my life, as I mentioned very early in the book, andragogy, or the methods of teaching adult learners or adult education. Obviously, I value education; it's a passion of mine. However, in the business of electronics and in the business of just about everything, the letters after a name are nice—but actually being competent at a set of skills is even more important for most jobs.

In addition, for many positions in today's world, including electronics, a degree may not be necessary at all. There are many opportunities that can or should be based on core competencies, not necessarily a four-year degree and then even more training to get to baseline. Requiring a college degree for some jobs is a barrier to entry that may not (or should not) be needed, and requirements like that can keep industries from finding people to fill positions and this affects the pipeline.

For example, suppose someone is forty-five and has just been laid off. They have an associate degree from over two decades ago in something unrelated to your field. They are good with computers and have significant experience but don't have that degree. Perhaps they would like to come aboard your company. But your job description insists on a bachelor's degree. Yet this person is perfectly capable of—and has the core competencies for—doing this job. Yet they will be screened out. At the same time, you have problems filling this position. Also at the same time, because this person is forty-five, they have no intention of going back to college, spending a lot of money and also (most importantly, perhaps) lots of *time* to get that piece of paper.

> **Many of the jobs in today's electronics industry—as well as many industries in the United States and across the globe—should be built on core competencies, not degrees.**

This is a lose-lose proposition. Your company loses out on motivated individuals who want to join. The person, who might be very fulfilled and appreciative of the position, loses out on the opportunity.

In my opinion, many of the jobs in today's electronics industry—as well as many industries across the globe—should be built on core competencies, not degrees.

COMPANIES ARE NOT IN THE EDUCATION BUSINESS

Companies are not universities. They are not designed to educate, per se. They are designed to *train* (and often, not even that). Very often, the typical advice on how to educate people to perform jobs in your industry is to partner with a local community college or university. While this might be a piece of the puzzle of education, it's not the only—or even strongest—piece.

A college is not able to pivot or be proactive. It tends to be reactive—and *slowly* reactive at that. Positions are needed in *XYZ* company or industry; a degree program is devised to company *XYZ*'s specification; graduates are still *years* away from entering the industry, and by that time, the industry has changed. Or worse, the company the college partnered with may have shut a location or moved or even gone bankrupt—leaving graduates in a town or city or location with no obvious company to go work for.

Before your company designs a training program or thinks about educating people to join your organization, you must ask yourself some important questions:

- Who are the ideal partners for your company to train your employees?

- How do you develop excellent core competencies?

- How do you handle education internally? Is that the best use of those resources?

- How do you do it in a hybrid fashion?

- What does an effective training program look like?

- What problems does your training program solve?

- What does your company know about the science of learning?

- Where do you go to get help?

And the answer to many of these questions is "It depends"—you have different answers depending on what you need to train a person on and where they are in the training sequence.

CORE COMPETENCIES: THE TWO EXTREMES

First, I suppose we should define what "core competencies" mean. The most basic definition is that they are the defining capabilities and skills needed to do a job.

Most companies do not have core competencies in education. Instead, they often fall into one of two extremes.

The first is this: "Welcome aboard! Now go do the job." I suppose we might call this the "sink or swim" approach.

The problem is this assumes everyone who graduates from college with an engineering degree, for example, is ready to start work. Or that everyone transitions to new learning and duties in the same way. Most people in management in any industry will tell you this simply is not so.

The other extreme is this: "We are so different. We have to train you in *everything*. Every single aspect of our company, our way, down to the most minute element."

Somewhere in between those two extremes is the answer.

For example, a new employee, fairly green, such as a fresh graduate, is hired and is entering the workforce and new to the industry in their first job. That industry has standards and basic operating practices across the board. Your company can purchase already-designed training particular to the industry—broadly. Then you can have particular training or education applicable to your company, "the Acme way of doing things," using our fictitious company.

Let's use the welding industry as one case. In the welding industry, for someone to become a welder, it is understood that they need to go to the American Welding Society, get training, get certified, and then get hired by a company. That welding training they received to obtain their certification shows that they can now perform the basics of the job of a welder. Their credential is proof of that. But the green new welder will still probably have to prove themself to the company as part of their interview. Next, the company will ideally have a training program to show the new welder precisely what the company expects them to do as part of their onboarding.

Thus, one aspect is competence verification—the person has been trained and is capable of doing the job. The other is company specific. Can you do *our* job? Great, we'll show you how. This outside training is essential because no company wants to set up a welding school, a computer coding school, a robotics school within their facility. It's unwieldy and makes no sense.

Now let's look at a different example. An engineer has been working for five years at a company and is moving into a role of supervisor. As a senior engineer, now they've got their first team. This is probably the biggest gap in all of company education. This is because, in my experience, they've been on teams. They've been at the company. People think: "Obviously they know how to lead." But they don't. However, there are standard techniques to leading a team. And there are many ways you can provide this. One of the great tools, for example, is LinkedIn Learning (formerly Lynda.com, acquired by LinkedIn).

I remember I was at one of my companies, and we had promoted a fantastic person into leadership and supervision. She was phenomenal, and everyone agreed she was not only ready but was the right person for the job. After being told of her promotion, she immediately asked, "Wonderful. Now where's my training?" The funny thing was we had not thought of that per se—and here I was, a great believer in adult education and training.

There are some basic standard aspects to leading. There's no reason for you to have customized "how to be a leader" training, or specialized (unique to your company) training on "how to lead a meeting" or, for example, "how to lead a project"—there's project management, where you get certified as a Project Management Professional (PMP). You can even use training that is fairly short, narrow, and specific. You don't need to spend a week training on how to do an expense report for your company.

On the factory side of things, there are some general things that employees need to know. There's factory safety or your OSHA requirements or, in the electronics world, your electrostatic discharge (ESD)—all of these things are very standard. There is no need for your company to spend the time and the money developing training programs for this. But for each particular machine, there are nuances you'll need to know: "This machine will blow up the world if you push the wrong button" is a good thing to know.

The ideal is to have the right mix between the general and the specific. There is no need to reinvent the wheel.

IPC sets standards for the electronics industry and offers competency training. Some of the largest companies in the world use that training. The reason they do that is because they understand efficiency. They want our training to integrate with their systems. We have programs that we license to training centers, and they will train on our behalf. We are the credentialing body. And we do the test for an actual certification. On the skills front, we work with hundreds of industry companies to develop our programs. We have a fantastic team of instructional designers. They take the information from the industry and create the instruction using the latest learning science. Then we offer that in an asynchronous format or online live format. IPC actually certifies more people than most universities. Have you found a partner like IPC in your industry?

INTERNAL EDUCATION

Now that we've addressed core competencies, those things that can be taught across an entire industry, we can address internal education. This part of training or education is focused on what's unique to your company. With every aspect of training, you must keep asking the question: *Is this really unique to us?* Everybody thinks they're unique. Guess what? Everybody and certainly every part of your company isn't.

> Everybody thinks they're unique. Guess what? Everybody and certainly every part of your company isn't.

I will use an example from years ago at IPC. We were working with all of the aerospace companies, and generally, their attitudes were that they each had their own standards because they are unique. This might be an easy assumption to make since aerospace engineering is complex.

However, all aerospace companies have to deal with basically the same planes (sizes, types, etc.), the same kinds of vibration, the same kinds of thrust factors, the same elevation, etc. In actuality, 80 to 90 percent of the specifications, maybe more, are *exactly the same*. But because every company had their own specifications, companies that were trying to build parts for more than one company had to do everything separately.

IPC came in and, essentially, brought them all together and said, "We're all gathered here—and we are going to hash out the standards." And guess what? We could look at this specification or that and show all these companies that much of what they are doing is the same. So with their input, we created an IPC standard for the industry—and the companies could use that as a baseline and just cite the exceptions.

After this was done and the specifications were finalized, companies were able to say "Follow IPC specifications *X*, *Y*, and *Z*." Then, they could provide a set of specifications—a drastically smaller set—to say "This is how we do things for our specific plane." The trick is to determine what to do internally. You must really think about what your *truly* unique processes are. What is your set of machineries or requirements that are actually different? Not just proprietary—but fundamentally *different*.

HANDS-ON TRAINING

The specifications and training that IPC develops is knowledge training. What about hands-on training? Again, you are not entirely unique. You can still do the general parts of training in a general setting. Then you can send people (or train them in house) for that hands-on part so an instructor reviews how your trainees actually *do* something (not just learn something). Let's go back to our welding example. Your company needs to have people certified to weld. You might be able to get away with a virtual class—but it's a little tough. Perhaps someone might take a picture of their welding and send it in to the instructor. But that really doesn't prove the person knows how to weld. How do you know it is even their work? Or isn't a photo lifted from the internet? Instead, you need to send someone to a place where they can actually weld and where someone who is qualified to judge that welding is a witness and verifies welding is acceptable. An instructor then is verifying the workmanship.

Now the question often comes: Why wouldn't a company go to a community college to set up a program for potential employees to obtain this sort of verification? If it is something general, that may work. But oftentimes, companies go to a community college, and they work directly with them to say "We'd like you to create this class for us. When students graduate, we can hire them." For example, I know of a course designed to develop employees for a pharmaceutical company's manufacturing plant. Here's the problem I alluded to earlier in the chapter. A company usually is trying to hire somewhere between 5 and, say, maybe 150 people certified for that specific skill in a specific location. They are creating their own pipeline. Isn't that great—what I've been advocating for in the book? In this case, it's not ideal. Once they've trained those people, now they have a college or university that's only localized and that has specific knowledge that now has no students for that and no more jobs—they've been filled.

On the other hand, it does pay to do those local partnerships in a different manner. For example, IPC has training centers that we partner with. The content comes from the electronics industry and is broadly applicable to that industry. That's where the input from many companies (like the aerospace example) is ideal. When we bring lots of opinions to the table, the product will be better—we are getting input and feedback from a variety of sources. People then exit the designed program with a certification or credential. Then you can take those same people to your specific factory and to your specific machine. You can point out "You learned *XYZ* skill in the classroom. Now this is our process where you can actually apply that. And now, there is 10 percent more to learn—the part of the job that is unique to us here at Acme. Our specific machine or process."

Germany does this very well. They have a very famous system implemented by the Fraunhofer Society. It's a research organization with roughly seventy-five institutes spread throughout the country; each institute focuses on different fields of applied science.[122] Students alternate between semesters of school and semesters of work—and by the time they graduate, guess what? They are competent and ready to work, less "green" than college graduates in the United States.

INTERNSHIPS AND APPRENTICESHIPS

In the United States, we have internships and apprenticeship programs. Internships often work out well—the intern has the opportunity to work in a company and in a position and see if it's a fit. The company gets to try them out, and if it's a match, the intern is often offered a full-time job at the end of the internship. Apprenticeships (often with funding from the federal government) do provide an opportunity for the apprentice to learn—but they learn skills and then may move on. It is not as wedded to the company.

Why can't the United States create something like the Fraunhofer Society? While I am sure there are many factors contributing to this, one issue is cities, states, and regions tend to watch out for themselves. Another is that education is the purview of the state, not the federal government. Finally, the Fraunhofer model is largely funded based on commissions—without measurable success, they don't get paid. Education systems in the United States don't seem to orient on delivering work capabilities as outcomes. The United States is a large country, and we are united in some ways. But states and cities often compete against each other (including offering tax incentives and other enticements) to attract a company to their location (and thus the jobs that would bring) instead of saying "Let's establish a nationwide program and set of institutes that benefits people across all fifty states." An example would be when Amazon looks to establish a new warehouse. They are essentially looking for the city or location that offers them the most—in both incentives and population.

STACKABLE CREDENTIALS

Ideally, you will want credentials to be "stackable." For example, when IPC reached out to our industry, we in essence asked, "What jobs do you need filled? What skills do people in those positions need?" We listened to our members, and we collected information from hundreds of companies. One example is the position of an inspector.

As basic as that position sounds, we first had to ask "What's an inspector?" Everybody had a different definition, often subtle differences. So we worked with the industry and defined what an inspector is, and then the industry shared the skill set that would enable someone trained and certified by IPC to have the best chance at a number of jobs or positions.

Next, we start with the basics—the simplest and broadest skills and training needed. Then, like building blocks, we stack more skills on top of that, more certifications. Let's take the simplest case. I'm a production employee. What do I need to do to work in production? Based on our in-depth study of our industry, we created a program for the most basic form of that (for example, placing parts on a board). Generally, robots and machines do that actual work of placing the parts. But ensuring the robot is set up correctly, reviewing the work the robots have done, and inspecting it are the basic skills needed. Potential production employees then need to pass that course. (It might take two hours, it might take two days, it might take two weeks, depending on the skill being learned.) This is the beginning of their career pathway! If someone wants to move to the next level of production or move on to a higher position, there are additional modules they can complete. This is how they stack or build the credentials they need.

What we need to be focusing on is the core competencies needed to continue to develop new skills and then provide expertise to get the upskilling. Universities do a great job on the fundamental skills and to some degree they can provide some upskilling opportunities. But the problem is the long length of the courses. It takes years, not weeks or days. If a company partners with a university, their first new employees will be at least four years away.

Industries that do a great job of using credentials find ways to bring individuals with known quantities of skills to their workplaces. In addition to knowing what you are getting, as you can see from the illustration below, industry credentials and certifications help individuals find more lucrative positions.

Credentials

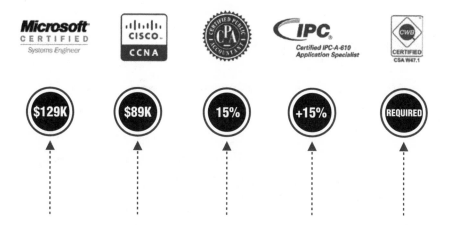

Figure 8.1: Credentials increase the value of the employee who holds them [123]

ONLINE AND VIRTUAL LEARNING

As someone in the electronics industry, I'm around cutting-edge advancements all the time. Artificial intelligence, robotics, additive processing, etc. But beyond what we're actually building, advanced technology helps us teach and certify people. For instance, I could create a class and release it online and potentially I can teach tens of thousands or hundreds of thousands of people all at once. This is highly efficient.

At some point, it is logical to assume that the "hands-on" training I referred to earlier could be done with virtual reality. I ask you to press a button as a production employee, and you actually "press" it but in the virtual world. At some point, we will see breakthroughs for mainstream adoption of such—even though the technology is available, it isn't mainstream or cost effective. Yet.

DON'T FORGET HIGH SCHOOL

Engineers, those in the C-suite, managers ... we expect to find those people with college degrees (at least in most Westernized systems). But the reality is that production and factory positions often need to be filled in very large numbers. For example, I toured a company in China that was in need of five hundred production workers.

You are not likely to find production workers on LinkedIn, for example. One place to find production employees are community colleges and high schools. Right now in the United States, we have created an education system that tends to focus solely on getting kids into college. Worse, much worse, is that society often makes those not going to college feel like failures. We don't celebrate kids going into a plumbing apprenticeship, for example. We often make community college feel "less than" a private university or large state university.

Yet these students are great, smart, capable people with potential. To remedy this attitude, what you need to do is find local opportunities to build on your pipeline and educate from there. If there is a trade association or a local high school near your factory, you can get in touch and ask whether they would be willing to have some of your people come in and talk about opportunities with your company. A dynamic speaker and sharing the realities of today's modern, clean, technology- and AI-driven factories, as well as the career paths in those factories can be exciting for the right students. Those who are interested can be invited to the factory for a tour.

There are other simple ways to generate interest. For example, you can sponsor a scholarship for five hundred dollars—not for college but to get training. You may recall that showing people *pathways* is important—as is quick training to get people onboard and working and collecting a paycheck as soon as possible.

If a high school student or community college grad is directly brought into a company at a production employee level and sees a pathway (and follows it), if the company constantly offers training and support as far as bringing this employee in, onboarding them, offering upskilling opportunities, and training them in new capabilities, employees develop a sense of loyalty to the company because they're taken care off and they can see a future. In fact, a McKinsey study showed that 35 percent of employees who leave do so because of not seeing career development or advancement opportunities.[124]

🔑 KEY CONCEPTS ———————————————————

Education is absolutely essential to finding and retaining talent. To review:

- Companies are not in the education business.

- In order to create a training or education program, you must determine what core competencies are needed and whom to partner with in order to create your pipeline.

- Avoid the two extremes of core competency training—sink or swim and handling all training on all things in house.

- Know that your company and competencies are not fully unique (in fact, very few competencies may be unique).

- Obtain broad training from outside sources.

- Use internal training for that which is truly unique and specific to your company.

- Figure out what requires hands-on training.

- Use internships as a way to "try out" a potential new employee—and vice versa (let them check you out as well).

- Ensure credentials are stackable.

- Do not forget high school and community college as sources for certain positions.

ACME AND NEW CO.: EDUCATION APPROACHES

✖ ACME'S EDUCATION WOES

Acme needs a hundred operators. And needs them now! (Yesterday, actually.) They put ads on Indeed and a few employment websites. To no avail. So Acme decides to partner with the local community college.

Acme's team spends six months developing a course that will train students on their particular needs, and they call it the Anvil Production Program. The course is designed to be taught over two semesters. At the end of the program, students are virtually guaranteed a job because they have been taught the Acme Way.

In the meantime, Acme is undergoing some changes (new equipment and technologies are integrated into the plant) and the program becomes slightly outdated, but the company knows they can retrain the graduates. Eighteen months later, the first graduates are ready (after six months of course design and two semesters of courses or training). After all this work, it only fills thirty positions. Unfortunately, the lack of operators results in a key factory line shutting down.

✔ NEW CO.'S NEW WAYS

New Co. needs over a hundred operators because they are expanding due to their success. They focus on three areas to find and train people:

- They do an open house, offering free pizza and a raffle for a new PlayStation game system, advertising it at the local high school on Career Night. They explain to the students that

New Co. has a hands-on training program. If they apply to work there after graduation (eight weeks away) and are hired, they will be able to be working on the line within four days and collecting a paycheck from day one.

- New Co.'s CEO writes an op-ed piece and also appears in several newspaper and magazine articles, and a few radio interviews discussing how senior citizens are going to be an integral part of their company. It's explained that many production and other positions do not require walking a football-field-sized warehouse, or other aspects of physical labor that may be problematic for seniors. The CEO discusses flextime, as well as all of New Co.'s wellness benefits. After these media appearances, New Co. sees an uptick in those over sixty applying for jobs.

- New Co. visits several community colleges and two HBCUs to discuss a new internship program. The program is a paid one, and New Co. makes clear that there is tuition assistance for stackable credentialing.

CHAPTER NINE

THE FUTURE IS NOW

A Vision of the Modern Workplace

Your future is whatever you make it, so make it a good one.
—"DOC" BROWN, *BACK TO THE FUTURE*

This book has covered much of what your hiring and employment practices *could* be. Some of these efforts may seem a little idealistic to some readers, but I want to assure you that this view of the modern workplace is not just some fantasy that is unattainable. This future is now. As we discussed in chapter four, there is an almost immediate loss of memory of the things we learn. And we have provided many such learnings throughout the book. To give a memory aid, I have tried to do a few things to enhance the retention of the material:

- I have summarized each of the key points made at the end of every chapter.

- I have provided stories to help solidify themes and expectations for most of the nuggets.

- And now, I am offering a simplified framework that can be reviewed (or downloaded) to trigger your memory and be used as a quick reference guide to the messages I've shared.

Let me quickly walk you through this framework, which we will call "Finders/Keepers Flow," as we are striving to either or both *find* the right people to join our organization and *keep* them and the critical staff.

As I walk you through several of these themes, let me use real examples, as opposed to the fictional ACME company we have used thus far. This is to further illustrate that the future is now. Every single thing I have explored in this book is totally possible.

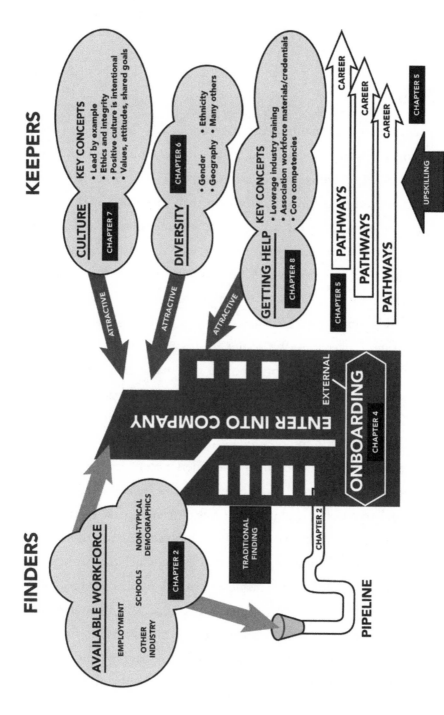

Figure 9.1: Finders/Keepers Flow

These are real-world examples of the principles of *Fire Your Hiring Habits*.

PIPELINE

In chapter eight, I mentioned the American Welding Society (www. aws.org). I wanted to tell you a little more about them and how remarkable they are as far as creating a pipeline. AWS listened to their members and codeveloped a study on their industry. (By the way, I hope you have noticed that listening is a key to so many of the parts of this book.) The study definitely showed that their industry was suffering from a dearth of skilled individuals entering the workforce. One reason for that, I am sure, is part of what was discussed in chapter eight. This country, in particular, has placed all its eggs in one basket: college and universities. We do not encourage our young students to enter into the trades—despite the fact that many trades will afford a higher income than some people with a four-year degree earn. One of the biggest issues is older welders were retiring and the average welder was firmly in middle- to later-middle age. Young people were not entering the field. Judging by the experiences of many I know, for example, on "career days," the emphasis is on "white-collar" jobs—you rarely see welders, plumbers, or electricians speak. Instead, the focus is on what's perceived as exciting, high-earning professional jobs (though a friend of mine was at a career day at which they brought in a dad who was a professional magician—you don't see that every day!).

Recognizing this was a significant problem in their industry, about a decade ago, AWS worked with their industry and government to develop programs and launch them across the United States to high schools, community colleges and training institutions. The challenge was to overcome a projected four-hundred-thousand-person welder deficit.[125]

AWS opted to build their own pipeline in a long-range plan (again, they began this process years ago). Similar to changing culture, where we discussed it being a multi-year process without quick fixes, they mapped out a strategy. They implemented this strategy by building the materials for training, the infrastructure for certification, and had faith that with these elements and outreach to high schools and community colleges, the people would come. Kids who liked to "work with fire"—an exciting prospect for some who want to work with their hands—could see a career path.

While the industry is still struggling, they now have a pipeline that takes those with an interest in the welding trade and helps them develop the skills to do the jobs the industry would like to hire into. The winners are everyone! The employers have people to choose from, the individuals who desire to wield that fire have a way to gain the skills, and the association has fulfilled their mission to safeguard their industry. The country wins too; jobs equal tax dollars, and the required infrastructure for a nation can actually be built.

Driving various sources of potential staff into your pipeline (AWS) or into your company training (discussed below) is the first part of the Finders/Keepers Flow (figure 9.1).

ONBOARDING

Indeed is considered by some to be one of the best companies for onboarding new employees.[126] One thing they do is bring their new hires together as a group across multiple departments (instead of, for example, all the customer service people onboarding together, and all of the website developers onboarding together). You can imagine that this helps create a cohesive whole for a company because instead of viewing each department as its own little pod, they are part of a bigger picture—and get acquainted with those from across the company. This creates "cross-functional" relationships from the outset.[127]

Another unique Indeed touch is the level of detail and guidance given to new employees. This includes step-by-step guidance and onboarding checklists.[128]

I personally know a new manager at Indeed, and indeed (pun intended), upon checking directly with him, they have great checklists and systems in place for him as a newly transferred-in manager. As he began hiring, he found that Indeed has made great investments in documenting and capturing action lists for onboarding so nothing that needs to be covered should be forgotten. These checklists get as specific as reminding managers to send certain emails a set number of days before someone is set to join the company and ensuring the contents of the email explain specific elements of the Indeed way. This helps ensure that the onboarding experience is consistent. It should not be that if you join Department A with Manager A, you are told one set of onboarding information, but if you join Department B, that manager forgets. The welcoming experience should include the same information and knowledge transfer across the company.

This kind of information transfer and "hand holding" during the early days of employment can set the stage for a positive experience as there are so many questions—even questions you don't know you should be asking as a new employee.

Onboarding without a pipeline is another challenge. If you are hiring and striving to develop the skills that will be needed, you will need an additional set of programs. IPC has worked with the leaders of the electronics industry to do just that. The Electronics Assembly for Operators program can take someone from the banking industry (there were several of those that seemed to be looking for new skills in prior downturns) and, in a matter of hours (not weeks or years), have them ready to be a productive employee and on the first step of their career pathway (remember that onboarding and pipeline education are the first steps on the career pathway—figure 3.2).

PATHWAYS

On one of my early visits to China as the CEO of IPC, I visited about a dozen electronics manufacturers. During these visits, we try to understand the challenges being faced by those companies, hoping that we can work with the industry to find solutions. To be a global leader, IPC cannot be myopically focused on only the United States. (Globally, China, the United States, and Germany are the top contributors to producing and exporting electronics.[129])

Every place I visited, I heard the same story: we have high personnel turnover. (Again, listening is a big part of determining how to fix any hiring/human resources problem.) The general gist of it was: "As soon as we develop some skills in our employees, they go across the street for a little more per hour, and we must start all over again!" This was shared with exasperation in their voices. This sort of frustration is a phenomenon nearly everywhere, though perhaps not at the same level of sheer numbers of people moving to new positions as in China for a variety of cultural reasons.

Near the end of my visit, I stopped by a Jabil factory north of Shanghai. Jabil, an electronics manufacturer, has over a quarter of a million employees, with one hundred plants in thirty countries.[130] I asked the same kind of questions I had been asking everywhere else, and I expected the same answers: that turnover was too high. While the folks at Jabil were concerned with employee turnover (as all companies should be), it was three to five times lower than the other manufacturers' facilities! I had to know more. What was their secret? Higher pay? Perks? The answer was fascinating.

They walked me down the hallway and showed me their progress board. This was a map of the various career pathways spelled out for all to see. Not only did the employees here understand where they could progress to, and how to get there, they had made those steps (to quote from *What about Bob?*) "Baby steps!" Every couple of weeks, an employee could move up the pathway toward their goal with increased skills, pay, and capabilities. They could literally experience their progress on that pathway just about every week as opposed to an annual review or later time frame. Who wouldn't be excited to see their career move along at that pace?

> **They could literally experience their progress on that pathway just about every week as opposed to an annual review or later time frame. Who wouldn't be excited to see their career move along at that pace?**

The result of this brilliant idea was loyalty and incredible cost savings with reduced turnover. There is much to be learned from this best-in-class direction. Was it easy to set up? No. Was it worth setting up? The proof was in just about every metric I can think of!

At the bottom right of the Finders/Keepers Flow diagram (figure 9.1), those arrows represent the path to a career that is clear and achievable for each team member. Remember, the better you define the rungs on the ladder to climb to the career goal, the more likely that staffer will know how to succeed with you and your company. Employees who know they have a future with definable goals and achievements are far more likely to come aboard and stay.

UPSKILLING/RESKILLING

Upskilling and education and reskilling in real-world companies can and should be part of the fabric of the corporate culture (see, again, how it all works together). The key point in the examples here is that these companies are continuing to invest in their employees' education and skills. This can take several forms. Some companies subsidize their employees' school degrees after hours or even during. Some provide free training via sites that we have discussed in the book like LinkedIn Learning. Some of these systems and perks aren't even limited to the employee but will extend to their immediate family as well. Talk about a loyalty generator. Here are a couple of examples:[131]

- Verizon calls their reskilling program Skill Forward. They provide both soft skills and technological training for their employees to develop their careers. Developed in partnership with Generation USA, a nonprofit working to transform education-to-employment systems, Verizon Skill Forward's free, fully online programs offer practical, hands-on learning experiences. Skill Forward participants can obtain free (who doesn't love that?), online (because this is very much part of the now and the future), and hands-on learning experiences (which makes them more memorable) in jobs such as: "Cybersecurity Analyst; IT Support Specialist; Junior Web Developer; Junior Full Stack Java Developer; Junior Cloud Practitioner; and Digital Marketing Analyst."[132] After completing the program, there are companies (including Verizon) waiting to hire the "graduates." Verizon Skill Forward is part of the company's $44 million commitment to training five hundred thousand workers for in-demand technology jobs by 2030.[133]

- McDonald's has its own education and upskilling program called Archways to Opportunity. This program offers employees education in bettering English language skills, free guidance, and help in obtaining high school degrees, tuition assistance for pursuing college degrees, and other services (like career guidance counseling). Since launching in April 2015, the initiative has supported nearly seventy-five thousand people and provided over $165 million in high school and college tuition assistance.[134] In its commitment to diversity and inclusion, McDonald's works with the Hispanic American Commitment to Education Resources (HACER) national scholarship program, as well as offering post-pandemic support programs for students enrolled at Historically Black Colleges and Universities (HCBUs).[135]

- Google joins forces with Jobs of the Future (JFF), a nonprofit, to train low-income adults for IT careers.[136] They offer an IT Professional Certificate program, including in areas like Appalachia and are another company dedicated to diversity and inclusion and equity. They also have a program called Grow with Google, which partners with existing nonprofits to provide skills training, including those who were incarcerated and now need a fresh start.

- Marriott (remember the Happy Marriott section?) makes our book again. They offer development programs, including the Global Voyage Leadership Development program for recent college grads in the Asia-Pacific region. The program focuses on key skills needed to be successful at Marriott, including culinary training, event management as well as accounting, finance, and human resources. The Marriott Development

Academy offers hybrid learning for career advancement and development. Within the Australian market alone, these programs have helped to fill over 55 percent of leadership positions with "hire from within" thinking and upskilling.[137]

CULTURE

Cultures that embrace flexibility, work-life balance, and growth of the individual (which actually benefits the company!) are able to attract top talent. But how do you develop a culture of innovation? Certainly, you can interview and hire people whose résumé and experience shows innovation—but that can be difficult to tell even in the most thorough interview. So innovation must be woven into the very fabric of a company. Enter Google.

When Google went public (2004), people began hearing about their "20 Percent Rule." Sergey Brin and Larry Page wrote:

> "We encourage our employees, in addition to their regular projects, to spend 20 percent of their time working on what they think will most benefit Google. … This empowers [our employees] to be more creative and innovative. Many of our significant advances have happened in this manner."[138]

> By this they mean 20 percent of the time should be dedicated to innovation—without necessarily seeing immediate reward. As with several aspects of this book, this is about a long-range view, as well as supporting creativity. Out of this thinking, successful outcomes of this mindset included Gmail, AdSense, and Google News.[139]

To revisit a topic I raised in the culture chapter, yes, work and religion can be part of a culture—*not* in the sense of requiring prayer, but instead in the sense that this should not be something taboo. It recognizes that a little less than half of Americans consider themselves to have a religious affiliation. (This is shrinking as the US population becomes more secular, but a quarter of Americans consider themselves spiritual without being religious—so spirituality is a part of many of our makeup.)[140]

The Religious Freedom & Business Foundation believes that religious freedom is good for business. They have approached the challenge of promoting this idea by talking the language of business. They have shown that organizations that promote and encourage inclusion and awareness of religion are more productive and profitable! Haven't met a business yet that didn't like the sound of those two words! The foundation talks about religious freedom as an aspect of "respect." But in addition to personal religious freedom, they mean in the larger sense that companies and businesses tend to avoid investment in places with religious suppression or a high level of religious conflict. This results in investment, instead, going to countries that respect the right of people of all faiths to practice that faith.[141] This fosters equity and inclusion. One example is the country of Eritrea. Roughly 6 percent of the population has fled the country. In particular, there has been persecution of Jehovah's Witnesses.[142] North Korea, other dictatorial countries, and suppressive countries are obviously not going to be candidates for global expansion in any business.

> You need a culture of respect, understanding, and learning. You need to continue to upskill your staff to make them better for your company and for themselves as individuals.

As you can see in the Finders/Keepers Flow (figure 9.1), culture impacts all aspects of solving the workforce challenges we face today. You need a culture of respect, understanding, and learning. You need to continue to upskill (figure 3.2) your staff to make them better for your company and for themselves as individuals. "Flow" means going from one place to another in a current—and that is the path you want to see, all of this working together.

PUTTING IT ALL TOGETHER

I hope you have garnered ideas for how you, too, can *Fire Your Hiring Habits* and evolve into the most modern, diverse, equitable, inclusive—and successful—company. From the very beginning of our journey with the "way, way back" time machine of human resources progress through new recruiting methods, the importance on onboarding to the progress in upskilling and reskilling employees, to addressing diversity, inclusion, equity, and culture, the modern workplace has never been more open to opportunities—though we still can go further.

I invite you to visit www.johnwmitchell.com to learn more about how to *Fire Your Hiring Habits*.

BUILDING ELECTRONICS BETTER

A Plan to Address the Workforce Challenges Facing the Electronics Manufacturing Industry

BY DAVID HERNANDEZ, CARLOS PLAZA, AND JOHN MITCHELL

WHO IS IPC?

As a global industry-driven organization, IPC exists to help its member-companies innovate, compete, and succeed. By being the hub of knowledge in the electronics industry, IPC provides standards, training and certification, industry intelligence, education, and public policy advocacy to help member companies achieve their goals. We are here to help our members create better-quality products, enhance the skills and knowledge of their employees, reduce costs and waste, comply with regulations, and be ready to capitalize on what is next.

Born out of the desire to transform the electronics industry more than sixty-five years ago, IPC became the voice of what was next—the breakthrough technology of printed boards. Today, IPC remains that voice as it continues to guide the electronics industry through dramatic changes. With more than three thousand member companies, IPC represents all facets of the industry including design, printed board manufacturing, electronics assembly, advanced packaging, and testing. Our goal is to help our members achieve financial and operational business success. We help the world build electronics better. One of the critical elements to a company's success is the ability to have a well-trained workforce.

A HOLISTIC VIEW OF THE ELECTRONICS MANUFACTURING WORKFORCE CHALLENGE

There is no singular workforce problem. Most of the rhetoric and literature surrounding workforce development focuses on a singular facet: *a gap between the knowledge and skills of the current workforce and the evolving needs of industry.*

While the skills gap is a significant challenge to the electronics manufacturing industry, it is a symptom of deeper-rooted challenges. The current workforce landscape for electronics manufacturing in the United States is a byproduct of four key failures:

1. The lack of an industry-driven talent *pipeline* that shifts the training burden from academic institutions to industry.

2. The lack of effective and efficient *onboarding* programs to rapidly bring new or under-skilled talent to full productivity.

3. The lack of a career *pathways* system to keep industry members engaged in their careers and foster the potential for growth.

4. The lack of a rapid *upskilling* infrastructure that helps the industry remain relevant in the face of relentless technological evolution.

Other areas of the world have overcome some of these challenges, but to one degree or another, these are global failures. IPC is working with the electronics industry to overcome these foundational challenges.

The purpose of this appendix is to present a holistic view of the workforce challenges facing the industry and outline IPC's approach and solutions.

THE PIPELINE PROBLEM

School-to-industry pipelines employ a variety of methods that work together to expose students to a field of work and provide opportunities for job candidates to acquire the necessary competencies in that field.

Promotional videos, career portfolios, interviews, demonstrations, and industry-related experiential activities are just some of the ways that pipeline advocates at schools and career centers introduce guidance counselors, parents, students, and other potential employees to the career opportunities in a given industry. Having identified interested candidates, the organizational members of a pipeline (e.g., schools, trade associations, government agencies, businesses) offer training, mentorship programs, internships, and other learning opportunities that prepare future workers to take on specific roles in the industry. Pipeline program graduates earn recognized, stackable, and portable credentials that allow employers to easily and accurately assess their level of competency and commitment to the field.

Schools and career centers with well-established pipeline programs can continually and reliably feed work-ready talent into an industry. Unlike manufacturing sectors such as machining, welding, and automobile maintenance and repair, the electronics industry is not well represented in academic and vocational curriculums. This leaves much of the career-specific educational process in the hands of companies with little or no academic expertise and significantly reduces the number of work-ready job candidates available for employment in the electronics manufacturing industry.

The lack of a well-defined and widespread school-to-industry pipeline exacerbates the challenges precipitated by accelerated retirements, a widening skills gap, and geographic imbalances of labor. It also poses recruitment challenges unique to the skill level of the positions that electronics manufacturers seek to fill.

PRODUCTION LEVEL. At the production level, the electronics industry relies upon a constant influx of mostly unskilled and untrained talent to fill the role of operator. In lieu of an education-to-employment pipeline, companies in an already highly competitive world market are tasked with recruiting and training responsibilities that cut into already-thin profit margins and skew the market in favor of organizations that can already afford them.

Electronics manufacturers that need to recruit production-level employees outside of a school-to-work pipeline must rely on career placement services, local partnerships, and public services, which may not be geographically or financially feasible. Moreover, effective in-house capacity to train new workers in both basic manufacturing (e.g., taking measurements, reading assembly instructions, interpreting tolerances) and industry-specific skills necessitates the recruitment, training, and supervision of learning development specialists. Recruitment and training of frontline employees is further complicated by the fact that numerous industries compete for a share of the same unskilled labor pool. Wage, benefits, and attrition rates track upward as electronics manufacturing companies vie with businesses from different industries for the same entry-level workers. With comparatively lower wages, limited opportunities for advancement, and comparatively high skill requirements, electronics manufacturing companies are losing current and potential workers to other industries. Continued electronics product price pressure from a global manufacturing base drives electronics production-level jobs to pay less than low-skill retail jobs per hour (and those positions often include benefits such as college tuition).

MIDSKILL LEVEL. Midskill-level technicians are responsible for programming, operating, and maintaining automated systems. These positions are gaining increasing relevance as automated technologies continue to take over the highly repetitive, low-skill tasks of the operator. The projected threefold to fourfold increase in industrial automation over the coming decade will give electronics manufacturers the precision, speed, and efficiencies required to deliver ever more sophisticated high-reliability products at competitive profit margins. However, unlike production-level operators who can be brought up to speed with a limited amount of initial training, the knowledge and skills required of technicians entails a significant investment—for both employers and job candidates.

Given the technical complexity and extended duration of technician training programs, electronics manufacturers are best served by school-to-industry pipelines composed of industry trade associations, industry members, schools, and relevant government agencies. Without a well-established midskill-level pipeline, electronics manufacturers are forced to compete for veteran workers capable of fulfilling these roles and invest scarce resources on in-house upskill training.

ENGINEER LEVEL. Electronics manufacturers face different recruitment and training challenges when it comes to the engineers involved in the design, fabrication, and assembly of PCBs, advanced packaging, and wire harnesses. Various industry sectors (e.g., aerospace, medical, automotive) compete for the limited number of engineers entering the workplace every year. Many of these sectors offer intra- and extracurricular pipeline programs designed to expose engineering students to potential career opportunities. Individual companies in different industry sectors also partner with schools to provide apprenticeship programs that allow engineering students to gain valuable work experience and build relationships with potential employers. Some of these sector- and company-specific recruitment and training efforts meet with success. However, industry-level school-to-work pipelines are able to cast recruitment nets across a much wider area and provide training and certification programs that substantially increase the diversity and quality of job-ready engineers across all sectors of the electronics manufacturing industry.

THE ONBOARDING PROBLEM

An industry workforce pipeline that consistently provides work-ready talent significantly increases the pool of qualified job candidates and allows member companies to scale production as needed. In a well-structured workforce pipeline, academic institutions such as high schools, trade schools, community colleges, and universities provide basic industry knowledge and skills. This educational foundation then allows employers to focus on company- and role-specific employee training.

This symbiotic relationship between the academic and commercial sectors is win-win. Companies reduce the time it takes for employees to achieve full productivity and thereby decrease the costs associated with extended times to proficiency. They are also able to reduce costs on learning and development programs that are more effectively handled by academic institutions. Productivity increases and cost reductions incentivize companies to support the academic institutions that provide job-ready employees. This support often comes in the form of funding, donations of material and equipment, access to facilities and professionals, and feedback on the effectiveness of academic programs.

A well-functioning workforce pipeline therefore relies on the expertise of two pivotal social institutions: academic institutions and manufacturing organizations. Academic institutions shoulder the majority of the fundamental training responsibilities because their core competency is education. This allows manufacturing organizations to focus on specialized training that helps to ensure the financial success required to continue to invest in these same academic institutions.

The lack of a workforce pipeline shifts the educational responsibility from academic institutions to employers. This challenge is compounded because most manufacturing companies do not count training among their core competencies. Those companies without preexisting educational infrastructures capable of offering extensive new hire training must rely on inefficient and ineffective strategies, such as shadowing, or invest heavily in the development of internal training capabilities.

The lack of a workforce pipeline poses an even greater challenge to the industry as a whole. Organizations without access to the standardized educational programs normally delivered by the academic partner in a workforce training pipeline are driven to develop individualized solutions focused on immediate needs and specific processes. Deprived of a substantial portion of the industry's foundational knowledge and skills, employees trained in this manner are limited in their role as employee and cannot readily advance. Given their narrow training and limited opportunities for growth, these employees are likely to resign within a short period of time and leave the industry altogether.

This is the worst possible outcome from an industry-wide point of view. While no employer wants to lose employees to potential competitors, the migration of qualified workers from company to company within a single industry (intra-industry attrition) ensures the availability of job-ready candidates that industry members can draw from to scale their operations as needed. In contrast, all industry members lose when employees migrate to other industries (inter-industry attrition).

THE PATHWAYS PROBLEM

The lack of standardized foundational training in the electronics manufacturing industry increases the time it takes a new employee to reach full productivity and limits their potential to fill new roles when the need arises. Just as importantly, inadequate training also limits an employee's potential to grow within their field. Where there could have been an employee inspired by the prospects of a *career* in electronics manufacturing there is instead a worker who does a *job* for the highest bidder. Both inter- and intra-industry attrition is higher among the latter. In fact, studies show that nearly 37.9 percent of employees who don't receive the training required to perform effectively will leave their positions within the first year.

To be sure, factors such as a person's background, experience, and age play a role in the way that they perceive the value of working for a particular employer or industry. However, a growing percentage of people prefer to work for companies who provide educational opportunities that facilitate advancement. For example, in a 2018 global analysis of the forces shaping the workforce of the future, 52 percent of millennials cited potential for career growth as the most important characteristic they look for in an employer.[143] A 2016 Gallup survey reported similar findings with 59 percent of millennials, 44 percent of Gen Xers, and 41 percent of baby boomers identifying training and growth opportunities as important considerations when applying for a position.[144]

More recent research indicates that this generational demographic trend became more widespread and pronounced during the recent spike in staff departures known as the Great Resignation. According to the US Bureau of Labor Statistics a historic high of over 47 million Americans voluntarily quit their jobs in 2021.[145] In a March 2022 Pew Research study, 63 percent of those surveyed said they quit their job in 2021 because their employer did not provide opportunities for advancement.[146]

The Great Resignation probably came as no surprise to Andrew Chamberlain. Citing his company's 2017 study on attrition in the Harvard Business Review, the chief economist and senior director of machine learning for Glassdoor noted that "even after controlling for pay, industry, job title, and many other factors, we find workers who stay longer in the same job without a title change are significantly more likely to leave for another company for the next step in their career."[147] When you consider that the median cost of turnover amounts to 21 percent of an employee's annual salary,[148] it's surprising that more companies do not take Chamberlain's advice to "provide clear paths for employees, moving them through job titles on a regular progression over time."

Career pathways are valuable:

- They chart the route an employee takes from an entry-level position through successive roles to arrive at their ultimate goal.

- The best occupational roadmaps allow employees to quickly discern the knowledge, skills, and experience required to perform a specific job.

- Clear pathways show how the acquisition of those competencies can help workers prepare to perform the next, usually more complex, role in a given field.

Sure, it seems logical for each company to develop their own career pathway framework, but this limits its effectiveness for employees, individual businesses, and the industry as a whole. The lack of a standardized industry-wide career framework that encompasses all of the essential roles in the electronics manufacturing industry (e.g., operator, technician, PCB designer, manufacturing engineer, program manager, etc.) limits the effectiveness of the training that academic institutions in industry pipeline partnerships impart to the students slated to eventually perform each of these essential roles. Different ideas about the attributes, scope, and qualifications of each role make it difficult for companies across the industry to accurately assess job candidates.

In contrast, a well-developed industry career framework includes industry-defined training and certification options that allow employees to demonstrate the acquisition of competencies at each stage of their professional journey. Employers that provide for these independently administered, stackable, and portable credentials help ensure both the proficiency and longevity of their workforce.

THE UPSKILLING PROBLEM

The lack of a standardized training infrastructure limits the industry's ability to rapidly and effectively upskill the current workforce in response to new technologies, processes, and standards. Part of the problem is the traditional teacher-centered instructional method that most industry members employ. This "sage on the stage" approach to teaching presents three primary challenges.

1. A live instructor limits the number of students in each class if they have any hope of effectively addressing the needs of the diverse groups of learners that we typically see in corporate training environments. Therefore, the only way to effectively scale this mode of training is to increase the number of trainers or increase the number of class sessions, and both solutions represent significant opportunity costs in terms of time and money.

2. The teacher-centric mode of instruction is born of our natural inclination to increase class size in an effort to maximize instructor productivity and reduce training lead times. Unfortunately, this ostensibly logical approach leads to significantly diminishing returns. Large class sizes reduce student achievement in most learning environments. One reason is that an instructor with more than a given number of students at a time cannot ensure that everyone in their class achieves the desired learning objectives. People—especially those of different ages, backgrounds, and language abilities—learn at different rates, and the time-limited, teacher-centered mode of instruction is simply not designed to help those who can't keep up. This mode of instruction caters to the mean, not the individual. This instructional limitation is

further compounded by the fact that learning is usually most effective when students engage in both guided and independent application of the concepts discussed in class. As you can imagine, an instructor already time-pressed to ensure the conceptual learning of their lowest performers will have little time left over to provide students with opportunities to practice their newly acquired knowledge and skills.

3. In a traditional class, students must sit through the prescribed program of study, regardless of their current understanding and experience. Not only does this waste valuable time and money, but it also dramatically undermines the student's faith in the efficacy of future training programs. In contrast, students that are given the opportunity to demonstrate their current competencies can focus solely on topics in which they need to learn or improve. This adaptive approach reduces training lead times and increases student engagement and retention.[149]

THE IPC APPROACH

The workforce challenges facing the electronics manufacturing industry are too broad and varied for any singular solution or approach. IPC believes that in order to address these challenges efficiently and effectively we must challenge many of the underlying assumptions that drive the current education paradigm. The heart of the IPC approach to the workforce challenge is that by challenging these assumptions and working in collaboration with the electronics industry, we can leverage technology and education best practices to make training solutions to address the four workforce challenges outlined by this appendix in an engaging, effective, and efficient manner.

COLLABORATION

The IPC education development process collaborates with industry members to produce standardized, industry-driven solutions that can be implemented at the organizational level to address their specific needs. IPC workforce solutions focus on the highest valued areas of skill and knowledge (which address the most critical industry needs). Instead of focusing on one specific industry, IPC seeks to understand the core problems affecting the industry as a whole. This is achieved by bringing diverse experts from throughout the industry together.

IPC's commitment to collaboration extends beyond the development process to the implementation of these solutions throughout the industry value chain. For example, addressing the pipeline challenges in the industry is predicated on the adoption of industry-recognized training and credentialing programs at the high school, community college, and university levels in order to both help build interest in careers in the electronics industry and prepare potential workers with in-demand knowledge and skills. Additionally, IPC recognizes that the challenges facing the industry without the support of key stakeholders. IPC is seeking to partner with governments at the local (state) and federal level to provide funding support for school implementation, industry training, and the development of programs to address emerging needs. IPC believes in total transparency, beginning with providing stakeholders with relevant and timely data regarding the effectiveness of these efforts and the vitality of the industries workforce.

SCALABILITY

The primary mission of IPC as the trade association for the electronics manufacturing industry is to help the world build electronics better. Throughout our history, IPC has never shied away from tackling the most critical industry problem regardless of scale. The numerous verticals that comprise the electronics manufacturing industry exacerbates the workforce challenges facing the sector as the needs of one vertical can differ from the needs of another. The varied needs of the industry necessitate scalable solutions. IPC's approach embraces the use of innovative educational technology to develop hybrid training solutions that blend the efficiency of online education and the specialized knowledge of industry trainers.

IPC recognizes that the needs of each organization differ. The programs developed in collaboration with the industry cannot provide the specialized knowledge and skill that are specific to each organization. Therefore, the program aims to provide 85 percent of the knowledge and skill needed to reach full productivity with the expectation that organizations will provide the company-specific knowledge. This partnership between industry and IPC allows for scalable solutions by lowering the barrier to effective and efficient training solutions that specifically address industry workforce challenges.

> **IPC training solutions are designed to be accessible to anyone, at any time, anywhere in the world.**

IPC training solutions are designed to be accessible to anyone, at any time, anywhere in the world. These programs generally require no preparation other than an internet-connected device allowing organizations to fill needs immediately without needing to develop or implement a new solution. IPC provides a variety of tools and services to training personnel allowing full visibility into student learning and progress, as well as access to the practice activity results and assessments. Through these tools, training personnel can manage learners and ensure their adequate progress in the programs. Additionally, IPC provides trainer guides for most programs, which provide optional, hands-on activities that can be implemented by companies to reinforce online learning. These activities are designed to be easily implemented with minimal disruption. By shifting the majority of learning to an online platform, trainers can ensure that each learner receives the individualized attention needed to ensure maximum learning retention.

EFFICIENCY AND EFFECTIVENESS

IPC Educational Developers use an instructional design technique known as scaffolding, which research has demonstrated improves overall learner retention while reducing frustration. This technique progresses learners through a variety of lessons, allowing them to master one set of competencies before introducing more complex information. The learner's progression is gradual enough to build their confidence while also keeping their interest by building on mastered information with more complex, difficult, or sophisticated learning. This allows learners to fully process one step or concept before moving on to the next. This is especially important when a step is essential to the understanding of a complete process or a concept is one of many required to grasp a given idea or topic.

The combination of scaffolding with the technology of the IPC online learning platform (IPC EDGE) allows learners to quickly progress through mastered information and to spend additional time on new concepts, thereby maximizing a learner's retention while minimizing the time spent learning.

In additional to scaffolding, IPC also utilizes a variety of other instructional techniques to drive learner efficiency and the effectiveness of the learning. For example, IPC utilizes a variety of media (audio, text, video, animation, and virtual simulation) to illustrate concepts, problems, and processes in a variety of ways, accounting for the spectrum of learning preferences. This learning is validated through regular, practical, and industry-relevant applications of that knowledge. These exercises and activities provide learners with meaningful opportunities to apply new knowledge or demonstrate their mastery. In project-based courses, such as the IPC Design programs, students are applying the knowledge gained into increasingly complex design projects that build on one another. These projects are evaluated by an IPC instructor, who subsequently meets with the student and provides feedback. In IPC asynchronous courses, where a live instructor is not available, students are asked to apply learning every few minutes to ensure understanding before moving to the next set of topics. This both ensures a deep understanding by the student (as they are able to apply the knowledge) as well as to keep learners from moving through the material too quickly (and thereby missing critical information).

IPC CORE BELIEFS

- **BETTER ELECTRONICS STARTS WITH BETTER TRAINING.** People are at the heart of every quality system. The training that an organization's team receives can either be a limiting factor or act as a multiplying effect.

- **COLLABORATION IN DEVELOPMENT, FLEXIBILITY IN IMPLEMENTATION.** IPC works closely with industry experts and learning specialists to create the most efficient and effective training experiences in the electronics industry. Industry SMEs help identify skills gaps, define the scope of training required to close those gaps, and ensure the accuracy of the content. IPC learning specialists then build learning experiences proven to facilitate the rapid assimilation and application of these new skills on the job. This powerful collaboration between the best minds in electronics manufacturing and instructional design allows IPC to deliver training that is more efficient because it focuses specifically on industry needs and more effective because it reduces the time required to assimilate and apply new learning on the job.

- **QUALITY TRAINING PRODUCES SUBSTANTIALLY MORE VALUE THAN COST.** Perennial problems, such as the lack of effective training programs, post-training performance support, and career pathways have led many electronics manufacturers to view new hire training and even veteran worker upskilling as a waste of time and money. When recently trained employees take positions with rival companies, some employers fail to consider other retention factors and "refuse to train their competitors' workforce." Of course, multiple case studies from industries as diverse as finance and manufacturing have shown that effective training programs (those that consider onboarding and performance improvement from the perspective of the worker, the work, the workplace, and the world) drive significant increases in performance and productivity *as well as* employee morale and retention. It also bears noting that a lack of investment in effective training eventually leads to a loss of revenue and market share. Companies with quality training programs simply outperform those that must bear the costs of rework, scrap, increased lead times, and other inefficiencies that inevitably result from trying to get by on one- or two-day knowledge dumps and trainee shadowing. Companies that invest in the efficient and effective training programs that IPC has created in collaboration with industry experts and learning specialists can expect a positive return in the form of:

- Reduced time to proficiency

- Reduced attrition

- Reduced training costs

- Reduced rework, repair, and scrap

- Increased product quality, reliability, and consistency

- Increased productivity

- Increased employee morale

THE IPC SOLUTION

Addressing the workforce challenges facing the electronics manufacturing industry requires the development of

1. a standardized, industry-wide workforce pipeline, and

2. a well-defined set of career pathways.

Without a school-to-industry pipeline to provide skilled, ready-to-hire employees, the burden of training shifts from academic institutions to individual companies that often lack the resources to effectively onboard and upskill new and current workers.

To address the immediate workforce challenges fueled by retiring boomers, persistent skills gaps, and post-pandemic shifts in worker expectations, IPC is working with industry to develop onboarding programs designed to help new employees rapidly acquire the knowledge and skills needed to reach full productivity.

At the same time, IPC will work with academic institutions to implement these industry-defined training programs across different levels of education. The resulting workforce pipeline will emerge over the midterm and long term as high schools, community colleges, and universities begin producing operators, technicians, engineers, and designers ready to join the electronics industry.

Of course, we won't solve the electronics industry's workforce problems if that new talent is lost to inter-industry attrition. Employees consistently cite career advancement opportunities as an important factor in accepting and staying at a job. That is why a career pathway system (CPS) helps mitigate the effects of attrition caused by factors such as pay and a competitive job market. A CPS maps the core competencies of key roles and uses this information to develop training programs that provide the skills needed to successfully perform each role. Workers whose employers actively use a CPS to help them plan and prepare for their next position begin to think about building long-term relationships and experiences instead of watching the clock and getting paid. In other words, employees begin to see their role in the electronics industry as a career instead of a job.

IPC is currently working closely with accomplished professionals across all sectors of the industry to delineate the competencies required to perform the roles critical to every company's success. For example, the CPS could be used to identify the academic pipeline programs, IPC workforce training courses, student internships, or on-the-job training designed to facilitate the transition from the role of tester to that of inspector or from the role of inspector to that of quality manager.

PIPELINE AND ONBOARDING

Educational pipelines are comprised of publicly available mechanisms that provide interested new and transitioning workers with the work-readiness and technical skills necessary to quickly contribute to an industry. This is not a novel concept. A variety of manufacturing and service industries rely upon well-established pipelines to minimize the training burden on industry, by increasing the available job-trained talent pool available to their industry. These pipelines often take the shape of standardized job-training programs and industry-recognized credentials that are offered through high schools, community colleges, career and technical training centers, and job-retraining centers. By offering job readiness and technical training, combined with the credentials recognized by the industry, these pipeline programs feed ready-to-work talent into the industry.

The lack of an industry-defined pipeline for electronics manufacturing in the United States has resulted in a growing talent gap. Absent a pool of ready-to-work talent prepared to enter the industry, electronics companies have resorted to hiring untrained workers and providing the basic skills and knowledge training after their hire. The shifting of the training burden to hiring organizations negatively affects the hiring organization by increasing costs (as the full training costs are borne by the company), decreasing productivity (by increasing the time between hire and the new employee reaching full productivity), and increasing their risk profile (as time, cost, and effort are expended by the company on unproven talent). This model also negatively affects the individual worker by reducing starting wages, limiting or extending out potential growth opportunities, and reducing potential learning time (and thereby reducing understanding and retention).

Therefore, business, industry, and government partnerships that provide the foundation for pipeline programs are critical for addressing the industry's workforce needs. IPC, as both the standards and certifying body for the electronics industry, is uniquely positioned to help address this need by working with industry to identify specific job and skill needs and develop programs that prepare new talent to meet those needs. For example, in 2021, IPC released a new workforce development program to prepare new assembly operators and wire harness operators for jobs in the industry by providing the knowledge and skill base necessary to perform the job function. IPC collaborated with over one hundred industry organizations to map and develop this program. In the last eighteen months, several thousand new operators entered the electronics manufacturing industry through these new programs.

IPC seeks to expand on the early success of these programs by collaborating with industry to develop a series of stackable education programs. These programs are grouped into three classifications:

1. Skill programs

2. Knowledge programs

3. Career exposure programs

Each of these program groupings is targeted at a specific workforce need. The IPC skill programs aim to provide the foundational competences necessary to perform skilled work within the industry at a variety of skill levels. Programs such as Introduction to Soldering provide the basic skills necessary to perform entry level soldering work, but also acts as the foundation for advanced soldering programs focused on rework and repair (which are areas of specific needs for the industry).

These skill programs are coupled with knowledge programs which build the theoretical understanding of core knowledge areas specific to each job role, as well as general knowledge areas such as electrostatic discharge and safety training. Building this foundational knowledge within the workforce is important for two key reasons. First, this knowledge is utilized by the workforce daily through the application of quality and reliability standards for electronics. Second, this foundational knowledge is important to the knowledge scaffolding necessary to perform more advanced jobs within the industry.

The final course grouping is focused on career exposure training. These programs are designed specifically to expose students and potential new workers to various career options in electronics manufacturing through in-depth exploration of day-to-day activities, video interviews and testimonials, and even simulated activities. These programs provide students with detailed looks into some of the most advanced and exciting portions of the electronics industry and demonstrates how they can be a part of a its future. But these programs are not just designed for students who are interested in entering the industry as a new worker. These courses also introduce groups of students that are not considering manufacturing work to careers they never considered. Makers, electronic and computer hobbyists, and students in robotics programs all utilize some of the same skills taught through the IPC skill programs. Providing these with access to this skill training and career exposure courses introduces an idea of careers in electronics in context of advancing their individual interests. Even students that are expecting to continue their education in community colleges or universities benefit both from the basic skills training and the early career exposure. For example, students continuing on to study electrical engineering can benefit greatly from soldering training, both because at the higher education levels they may need to solder as part of prototyping, but also as a means of contextualizing what they are learning.

IPC's plan is to utilize the same online learning platform utilized by the electronics industry around the world to distribute content to schools. This would allow schools to adopt the same education and credentialing programs utilized by the industry, while minimizing the start-up time for new programs. IPC seeks to combine online learning content with in-person practical instruction through a hybrid approach: the theory components are taught online with contextualization and simulation (which allows for more practical application without the need for equipment or additional cost), while furthering the practical application through hands-on activities and demonstrations. This will require that IPC provide instructors with access to materials and instructor training. Students that complete these programs are awarded IPC credentials to help illustrate their level of skill and knowledge to industry.

The industry pipeline will continue to grow over time (in both programs resources and in adoption), but it will not address the immediate problems that exist today in the industry. These programs take time to implement and grow. There is no single switch that activates a pipeline for the industry. Instead, this will require a continuing, concerted effort by IPC, industry, government, and schools over a period of years. Therefore, a short-term solution is needed while the long-term pipeline is established and implemented in enough schools to meet the long-term industry need. IPC believes that both solutions must be developed in conjunction. IPC is currently providing the industry with access to turnkey, asynchronous onboarding programs that can be implemented at the company level for incoming and transitioning employees. Some of these same programs will become the foundational stones of the future training pipeline.

Educational pipelines typically flow in a cyclical nature aligned to the educational cycles. Career and technical education programs at the production level may run continuously throughout the year depending on program length, but typically run cohorts of students through at the same time. Therefore, new talent only becomes available once a cohort completes a program. This is then followed by a period of time when new talent is not available. If each academic program ran their education cycles completely independent from one another, this would minimize the impact of these cycles. But schools tend to run along the same calendar cycles (plus or minus a few weeks), meaning that there will always be lulls when talent is not flowing into the industry. This is a more significant challenge at the technician and engineering level, where programs are typically tied to two-year or four-year education cycles, thereby limiting the flow of new talent to "graduation periods." Furthermore, not all students avail themselves of formal education programs. There are multiple pathways to enter the electronics manufacturing industry, of which schools are just one. For example, inter-industry migration of adult workers such as engineers, veterans transitioning to civilian life, etc. is quite common, particularly for high-skilled workers.

IPC is currently working with the electronics industry in developing onboarding programs at a variety of skill levels: operator, technician, engineer, etc. These programs are designed to teach 85 percent of what the new employee needs to know to be effective in their new role. The remaining 15 percent of knowledge is provided by the company (specific company processes, equipment, components, etc.). Currently available programs implemented by IPC member companies demonstrate a dramatic reduction in time-to-full-productivity by new employees that undergo this onboarding training.

In order to address industry-wide needs (instead of specific geographic challenges) IPC works with industry to standardize training programs. By crowdsourcing information, IPC also ensures that new talent entering the industry could produce value across the industry.

Standardization, however, does not imply rigidity. The IPC programs are designed to allow for flexible implementation to accommodate the needs of a diverse industry. For example, the assembly operator onboarding program is divided into mandatory and optional modules. The mandatory modules are those knowledge and skill areas that the industry has identified as being universally important regardless of the specific job role.

PATHWAYS AND UPSKILLING

The workforce challenges in the United States and many other parts of the world can be segmented into two broad categories: talent acquisition problems and talent retention challenges. Both the industry pipeline and onboarding programs provide mechanisms to draw new talent into the electronics manufacturing industry and help the talent reach a full level of productivity efficiently. Once the new talent is in the industry, how does the industry keep that talent in an increasingly competitive marketplace? The electronics manufacturing industry is burdened with preexisting negative attitudes toward manufacturing careers.

Without talent retention mechanisms, the electronics manufacturing industry will succumb to a cycle of continuous talent acquisition and training resulting in decreased productivity levels, increased costs, and a loss of tribal knowledge. Employees increasingly prioritize career growth and continuous training when evaluating potential employers and industries. IPC believes this is the heart of the attrition problem.

Shifting industry perspectives from jobs to careers requires both knowledge of potential future growth and access to the means of that growth. IPC identified the following roles in the industry as critical to long-term success:

- **PRODUCTION LEVEL:** Assembly operators, wire harness operators, PCB operators, assembly inspectors, PCB inspectors, trainers

- **TECHNICIAN LEVEL:** Manufacturing technicians, production technicians, design technicians, quality/test technicians

- **ENGINEERING LEVEL:** Production engineers, manufacturing engineers, PCB designers/design engineers, quality engineers

Individual career pathways are built from the data collected through industry job task analysis, competency mapping activities, and workforce development working groups. The process identifies the key competencies of each job role and the critical tasks to which they are mapped. When the requirements for a specific job function and the corresponding competencies vary significantly among those within the job role, then the competency maps will identify those variations. This typically occurs in two instances:

- If the job function of a role varies based on experience (i.e., as an individual's experience in the job grows, so do their responsibilities), then it is typically appropriate to develop levels to a particular job function. For example, the industry may differentiate the job functions of an inspector and a senior inspector to the point where they may be considered different jobs.

- If the job role varies based on application, then it is typically appropriate to differentiate the job roles by those applications. For example, IPC identified that the functions of an assembly operator and a PCB fabrication operator are fundamentally different, and the competencies necessary to perform this job vary to a large degree; therefore, they are categorized as two different types of operators.

Once competency maps for various careers are completed, then commonalities among necessary competencies help identify connected pathways. For example, if 30 percent of the competencies for career 1 and career 2 overlap, then an individual in a job function related to career 1 would need to obtain the 70 percent of required competencies for career 2 in order to transition to a job role related to that career. This plays two important functions:

- First, it clearly defines the knowledge, skills, and abilities that an individual would need to attain to transition to the new career and identifies the interconnectedness between those KSAs. This provides a "pathway" to obtaining their desired career growth.

- Second, by connecting the careers together in a pathway, the individual is able to recognize the competencies that already possess and therefore can focus on the 70 percent of new competencies they need to obtain to transition job functions.

Essential to this are certification programs, which

- establish minimum levels of proficiency with career specific competencies,

- ensure industry organizations of an individual's ability to perform their job effectively, and

- help the organization position the individual for future growth.

Most individuals will reach a point in their careers where growth to a new career role is no longer desirable. These individuals may instead seek to specialize their knowledge or to seek continuous education in advanced topics. Regardless of their individual goals, however, access to continuous education is the key to long-term relevance. As the industry and technology evolves, individuals must continuously update their existing skill set just to remain at the same level of competence. Without a means of easily disseminating this type of training on a wide scale, the industry will quickly trade one set of workforce challenges for another.

As the industry advances, IPC collaborates with forward-looking organizations to develop new upskilling programs for emerging technologies, materials, and processes. These programs are disseminated through the EDGE platform, allowing for the rapid upskilling of whole organizations or industry sectors.

Visit https://www.ipc.org/education-main-page for the latest happenings in IPC Education.

SCAN TO ACCESS THE DOWNLOADABLE
SUPPORTING DOCUMENTS, INCLUDING
COLOR VERSIONS OF THE DIAGRAMS!

ACKNOWLEDGMENTS

It would be impossible to recognize all the influences in my life that have helped shape my passion for education and making a difference. Instead of attempting the impossible and inevitably leaving someone off the list of my gratitude, let me instead highlight just a few of those who have helped to drive this specific work from a desire to reality.

Primary thanks go out to the IPC Board of Directors for their support in solving workforce challenges—they helped provide the vehicle that made all this possible. Additionally, David Hernandez for his undying passion in understanding, diagnosing, and providing frameworks to solve workforce challenges. I never thought I would find someone else who was as passionate about education and the impact it can make upon both an individual's life as well as a society as a whole.

Finally, to all of those teachers, educators, and advisors (both formal and not) who have not given up on trying to teach me to become better—in so many ways—I thank you for your specific instruction, and perhaps more importantly, your examples of perseverance, dedication, and desire.

ABOUT THE AUTHOR

Dr. John W. Mitchell is a thought leader who has transformed the way we look at advancing and resolving education, nonprofit leadership, and advanced manufacturing issues. As President and CEO of IPC, a global trade association representing all facets of the electronics industry, Dr. Mitchell has championed new solutions supporting standards development, improving member relations, advocating regulatory change, and new learning management platforms to address workforce issues.

An accomplished executive with a strong interest in the challenges facing management and education, Dr. Mitchell was a founding member of Alpine Electronics' U.S.-based research company credited for introducing navigation systems to the U.S. Original Equipment Manufacturer (OEM) market. He also served as general manager and director of a global business unit at Bose Corporation. Prior to joining IPC, Dr. Mitchell served as the CEO of Golden Key International Honor Society, the world's premier collegiate honor society.

Dr. Mitchell's academic credentials include a doctorate in higher education management from the University of Georgia Institute of Higher Education, a Master of Business Administration from Pepperdine University, and a Bachelor of Science in electrical and computer engineering from Brigham Young University. He holds a patent in GPS navigation systems and is a published author.

An accomplished triathlete and Ironman competitor, Dr. Mitchell lives with his family near Atlanta, Georgia.

ENDNOTES

1. Parth Misra, "Investing in Your Employees Is the Smartest Business Decision You Can Make," Entrepreneur, June 29, 2018, https://www.entrepreneur.com/growing-a-business/investing-in-your-employees-is-the-smartest-business/315095, accessed 10/6/2022.

2. Bureau of Labor Statistics, "Labor Force Projections to 2024," December 2015, https://www.bls.gov/opub/mlr/2015/article/labor-force-projections-to-2024.htm, accessed 10/6/2022.

3. Tradingeconomics.com, "China Job Vacancies—Forecast," accessed April 20, 2022, https://tradingeconomics.com/china/job-vacancies.

4. Eurostat, "Underemployment and Potential Additional Labour Force Statistics," May 2017.

5. PricewaterhouseCoopers, "US Remote Work Survey," accessed April 18, 2022, https://www.pwc.com/us/en/library/covid-19/us-remote-work-survey.html.

6. Ian Johnson, "China's Great Uprooting: Moving 250 million into Cities," The New York Times, June 15, 2013, https://www.nytimes.com/2013/06/16/world/asia/chinas-great-uprooting-moving-250-million-into-cities.html.

7. Wikipedia, "China Industrialization," accessed April 20, 2022, https://en.wikipedia.org/wiki/Chinese_industrialization.

8. Peter Evans and Sarah Stavetieg, "The Changing Structure of Employment in Contemporary China," 2009, IRLE Working Paper No190-09, accessed April 18, 2022, http://irle.berkeley.edu/working-papers/190-09.pdf.

9. D.M. Fisk, Bureau of Labor Statistics, "American Labor in the 20th Century," accessed April 18, 2022, https://www.bls.gov/opub/mlr/cwc/american-labor-in-the-20th-century.pdf.

10. Makiko Inoue and Ben Dooley, "A Job for Life, or Not? A Class Divide Deepens in Japan," *New York Times*, November 2020, https://www.nytimes.com/2020/11/27/business/japan-workers.html.

11. Rick Wartzman, "What Peter Drucker Knew about 2020," *Harvard Business Review*, accessed March 6, 2022, https://hbr.org/2014/10/what-peter-drucker-knew-about-2020.

12. Rani Molla, "The Pandemic Was Great for Zoom. What Happens When There's a Vaccine?," Vox, December 4, 2020, https://www.vox.com/recode/21726260/zoom-microsoft-teams-video-conferencing-post-pandemic-coronavirus.

13. IBM, "What Is Industry 4.0?," accessed April 19, 2022, https://www.ibm.com/topics/industry-4-0.

14. Seed Scientific, "How Much Data Is Created Every Day?," Seed Scientific, accessed April 22, 2022, https://seedscientific.com/how-much-data-is-created-every-day/#:~:text=How%20much%20content%20is%20created,2.5%20quintillion%20bytes%20of%20data.

15. Seed Scientific, "How Much Data Is Created Every Day?"

16. Bureau of Labor Statistics, "Employee Tenure Summary," September 2020, https://www.bls.gov/news.release/tenure.nr0.htm.

17. Bureau of Labor Statistics, "Employee Tenure in the Mid-1990s," January 30, 1997, https://www.bls.gov/news.release/history/tenure_013097.txt.

18. Gareth Sleger, "New Manufacturing Report Shows How Worker Turnover Costs the Industry," *Fabricator*, February 8, 2019, https://www.thefabricator.com/thefabricator/blog/shopmanagement/new-manufacturing-report-shows-how-worker-turnover-costs-the-industry.

19. Subhi Dani, "Employee Retention in China: Tips and Strategies to Increase It," August 3, 2020, https://www.hrone.com/blog/employee-retention-china/.

20. Marc Perna, "Under New Management: Millennials as Successful Managers," *Forbes*, accessed April 14, 2022, https://www.forbes.com/sites/markcperna/2020/08/11/under-new-management-millennials-as-successful-managers/?sh=4db087152248.

21. Michelle Fox, "What Gen-Z and Millennials Want from Employers amid Great Resignation," CNBC, May 18, 2022, https://www.cnbc.com/2022/05/18/what-gen-z-and-millennials-want-from-employers-amid-great-resignation.html.

22. A. Chamberlain, "What Matters More to Your Workforce Than Money," *Harvard Business Review*, January 2017, https://hbr.org/2017/01/what-matters-more-to-your-workforce-than-money.

23. Kavita Saini et al., eds., "Creating Pathways for Tomorrow's Workforce Today: Beyond Reskilling in Manufacturing," https://www2.deloitte.com/mt/en.html (Deloitte, 2021), chrome-extension://efaidnbmnnnibpcajpcglclefindmkaj/https://www.themanufacturinginstitute.org/wp-content/uploads/2021/05/DI_ER-I-Beyond-reskilling-in-manufacturing-1.pdf.

24. IPC International, "Findings on the Skills Gap in the U.S. Electronics Manufacturing," April 2017.

25. Andrew Deichler, "Help Wanted: Manufacturing Sector Struggles to Fill Jobs," SHRM.org, June 16, 2021, https://www.shrm.org/ resourcesandtools/hr-topics/talent-acquisition/pages/help-wanted-manufacturing-sector-struggles-to-fill-jobs.aspx.

26. "Professional Apprenticeships," accessed October 6, 2022, https://www.professionalapprenticeships.co.uk/ apprenticeship-or-internship-whats-the-difference/.

27. Ram Charan, "The Secrets of Great CEO Selection," *Harvard Business Review*, accessed April 24, 2022, https://hbr.org/2016/12/ the-secrets-of-great-ceo-selection.

28. Rebecca Schalm, "How to Use the 'Rule of Three' to Make Better Hiring Decisions," Troy Media, accessed April 21, 2022, https://troymedia.com/career-human-resource-information/ use-rule-3-make-better-hiring-decisions/.

29. Felipe Child et al., "Setting a New Bar for Online Learning for Higher Education," McKinsey.com, accessed May 15, 2022, https://www.mckinsey.com/industries/education/our-insights/ setting-a-new-bar-for-online-higher-education.

30. William Furey, "The Stubborn Myth of Learning Styles," *Education Next*, updated April 7, 2020, https://www.educationnext.org/ stubborn-myth-learning-styles-state-teacher-license-prep-materials-debunked-theory/.

31. Queensland Brain Institute, "How Are Memories Formed?," Queensland Brain Institute, accessed October 17, 2922, https://qbi. uq.edu.au/brain-basics/memory/how-are-memories-formed.

32. Art Kohn, "Brain Science: The Forgetting Curve—the Dirty Secret of Corporate Training," *Learning Solutions*, accessed May 12, 2022,

https://learningsolutionsmag.com/articles/1379/brain-science-the-forgetting-curvethe-dirty-secret-of-corporate-training.

33. Sean D'Souza, "How to Retain 90% of Everything You Learn," Psychotactics, accessed August 18, 2022, https://www.psychotactics.com/art-retain-learning/.

34. Tom Galvin, "What's the Difference Between an Apprenticeship vs. an Internship," Comptia.org, August 27, 2018, https://www.comptia.org/blog/what-s-the-difference-between-an-apprenticeship-vs.-an-internship#:~:text=from%20an%20apprenticeship.-,The%20best%20way%20to%20describe%20the%20difference%20is%20an%20apprenticeship,on%2Dramp%20to%20a%20career.

35. Kate Birch, "From the Mailroom to the Boardroom: CEOs Who Rose through the Ranks," *Business Chief*, accessed May 20, 2022, https://businesschief.com/leadership-and-strategy/from-mailroom-to-boardroom-ceos-who-rose-through-the-ranks.

36. Birch, "From the Mailroom to the Boardroom."

37. Subhi, "Employee Retention in China: Tips and Strategies to Increase It."

38. Zixi Liu, "Why Workers' Turnover Is So High: Managed Flexibility and the Intermediary Chain of China's Migrant Labor Market," *Journal of Chinese Sociology*, accessed May 27, 2022, https://journalofchinese-sociology.springeropen.com/articles/10.1186/s40711-020-00120-z.

39. Diedre Paknad, "How to Motivate Millennials at Work," WorkBoard, accessed October 6, 2022, https://www.workboard.com/blog/motivating-millennials.php.

40. Guy Berger, "Will This Year's College Grads Job-Hop More than Previous Grads?," LinkedIn, April 12, 2016, https://blog.linkedin.com/2016/04/12/will-this-year_s-college-grads-job-hop-more-than-previous-grads.

41. Harver, "10 Tactics to Reduce Employee Turnover in Manufacturing," Harver.com, accessed May 20, 2022, https://harver.com/blog/reduce-employee-turnover-manufacturing/.

42. Carla Tardi, "Moore's Law," Investopedia, accessed May 26, 2022, https://www.investopedia.com/terms/m/mooreslaw.asp.

43. Joe McKendrick, "AI Adoption Skyrocketed over the Last 18 Months," *Harvard Business Review,* accessed May 18, 2022, https://hbr.org/2021/09/ai-adoption-skyrocketed-over-the-last-18-months.

44. World Economic Forum, "Don't Fear AI: It Will Lead to Long-term Job Growth," World Economic Forum, accessed May 12, 2022, https://www.weforum.org/agenda/2020/10/dont-fear-ai-it-will-lead-to-long-term-job-growth/.

45. Scott Sorokin, "Thriving in a World of 'Knowledge Half-Life,'" CIO.com (CIO, April 5, 2019), https://www.cio.com/article/219940/thriving-in-a-world-of-knowledge-half-life.html#:~:text=In%201982%2C%20futurist%20and%20inventor,doubling%20every%2012%2D13%20months.

46. Mike Prokopeak, "Amazon Goes Big with 700 Million Reskilling Pledge," Chief Learning Officer, accessed May 20, 2022, https://www.chieflearningofficer.com/2019/07/11/amazon-goes-big-with-700-million-reskilling-pledge/.

47. Ben Wigert, "Top 6 Things Employees Want in Their Next Job," Gallup, accessed May 26, 2022, https://www.gallup.com/workplace/389807/top-things-employees-next-job.aspx.

48. Indeed, "The Importance of Employee Loyalty and How to Improve It," Indeed, August 11, 2021, https://www.indeed.com/career-advice/career-development/importance-of-employee-loyalty.

49. Wikipedia, "The Wisdom of Crowds," Wikipedia.org, accessed May 18, 2022, https://en.wikipedia.org/wiki/The_Wisdom_of_Crowds.

50. U.S. Department of Housing and Urban Development, "Diversity and Inclusion Definitions," HUD.gov, accessed May 20, 2022, https://www.hud.gov/program_offices/administration/admabout/diversity_inclusion/definitions.

51. Volvo, "Volvo Group Diversity and Inclusion Stories," Volvo Group, accessed May 15, 2022, https://www.volvogroup.com/en/careers/diversity-and-inclusion/diversity-and-inclusion-stories.html.

52. Volvo, "Volvo Group Diversity and Inclusion Stories."

53. Jeff Wild, "More Than 25 Major Companies Take the Innovation Diversity Pledge," IAM Media, accessed May 15, 2022, https://www.iam-media.com/article/diversity-pledge-25-companies-sign-usipa#:~:text=Adobe%2C%20AT%26T%2C%20Facebook%2C%20HP,that%20have%20made%20the%20pledge.

54. Ongig.com, "Five Examples of CEO Diversity Pledges," Ongig.com, accessed May 15, 2022, https://blog.ongig.com/diversity-and-inclusion/ceo-diversity-pledge/.

55. Glassdoor, "Two-Thirds of People Consider Diversity Important When Deciding Where to Work," Glassdoor.com, accessed May 26, 2022, https://www.glassdoor.com/about-us/twothirds-people-diversity-important-deciding-work-glassdoor-survey-2/.

56. Rocio Lorenzo and Martin Reeves, "How and Where Diversity Drives Financial Performance," *Harvard Business Review*, accessed May 26, 2022, https://hbr.org/2018/01/how-and-where-diversity-drives-financial-performance.

57. Corporate Leadership Council, "Creating Competitive Advantage Through Workplace Diversity," accessed May 26, 2022, https://s3.amazonaws.com/texassports_com/documents/2014/11/24/corporate_leadership_council_report.pdf.

58. John Kell, "Apple's CEO Time Cook: Diversity Is 'the Future of Our Company,'" *Fortune*, accessed May 26, 2022, https://fortune.com/2015/06/08/apple-ceo-diversity/#:~:text=Apple's%20CEO%20Tim%20Cook%20doesn,%2C%20I%20firmly%20believe%20that.%E2%80%9D.

59. Shannon Howard, "5 Diversity and Inclusion Quotes for the Workplace," Predictive Index, accessed May 26, 2022, https://www.predictiveindex.com/blog/5-diversity-and-inclusion-quotes-for-the-workplace/.

60. *Forbes*, "37 Business Leaders Who Spoke Out about Diversity and Inclusion," Forbes.com, accessed May 26, 2022, https://www.forbes.com/sites/forbesmarketplace/2017/12/18/37-business-leaders-who-spoke-out-about-diversity-and-inclusion-in-2017/?sh=386ff44d15a0.

61. *Forbes*, "37 Business Leaders Who Spoke Out about Diversity and Inclusion."

62. Todd Rose, "When U.S. Air Force Discovered the Flaws of Averages," *Toronto Star*, accessed May 28, 2022, https://www.thestar.com/news/insight/2016/01/16/when-us-air-force-discovered-the-flaw-of-averages.html.

63. Perna, "Under New Management: Millennials as Successful Managers."

64. Katharina Buchholz, "How Have the Number of Women CEOs in the Fortune 500 Changed in the Last 20 Years?," WeForum.org, accessed May 28, 2022, https://www.weforum.org/agenda/2022/03/ceos-fortune-500-companies-female#:~:text=2022%20is%20seeing%20a%20new,and%20only%207%20in%202002.

65. Buchholz, "How Have the Number of Women CEOs?"

66. Jennifer King, "Female CEOs in Manufacturing under 1.3%; Under 1% in Oil & Gas," *Pumps & Systems*, accessed

May 28, 2022, https://www.pumpsandsystems.com/ female-ceos-heavy-manufacturing-13-under-1-oil-gas.

67. King, "Female CEOs in Manufacturing."

68. Mike Musial, "How Can We Get Rid of the Glass Ceiling?," PMI. org, updated November 2001, https://www.pmi.org/learning/library/ women-workforce-better-than-men-7873.

69. Rhitu Chatterjee, "New Survey Finds Eighty Percent of Women Have Experienced Sexual Harassment," NPR.org, accessed May 14, 2022, https://www.npr.org/sections/thetwo- way/2018/02/21/587671849/a-new-survey-finds-eighty- percent-of-women-have-experienced-sexual-harassment.

70. Dan Avery, "Half of LGBTQ Workers Faced Job Dis- crimination, Report Finds," NBCNews.com, accessed May 22, 2022, https://www.nbcnews.com/nbc-out/out-news/ half-lgbtq-workers-faced-job-discrimination-report-finds-rcna1935.

71. Matthew Impelli, "More Americans Support LGBTQ Rights Than Ever Before," *Newsweek*, accessed May 26, 2022, https://www. newsweek.com/more-americans-support-lgbtq-rights-ever-before- poll-shows-1578261.

72. Bernie Wong, "Workplace Mental Health for LGBTQ+ Professionals," MindSharePartners.org, accessed May 20, 2022, https://www.mindsharepartners.org/post/ workplace-mental-health-for-lgbtq-professionals.

73. American Association of University Women, "The STEM Gap," AAUW.org, accessed August 22, 2022, https://www.aauw.org/ resources/research/the-stem-gap/.

74. Janice Gassam, "4 Ways to Build Your Company's Diverse Pipeline," *Forbes*, accessed April 27, 2022, https://www.forbes.com/sites/

janicegassam/2019/07/24/4-ways-to-build-your-companys-diverse-pipeline/?sh=5bb28e6e741b.

75. Gassam, "4 Ways to Build Your Company's Diverse Pipeline."

76. Mary Brophy Marcus, "Does Your Doctor's Age Matter?," CBSnews.com, May 17, 2019, https://www.cbsnews.com/news/doctors-older-age-patient-mortality/.

77. Great Place to Work, "100 Best Workplaces," Great Place to Work, accessed July 1, 2022, https://www.greatplacetowork.com/best-workplaces/100-best/2022.

78. Stephanie Chan, "Cisco Ranks as One of the Best Places to Work—Here's Why," Cisco.com, accessed April 27, 2022, https://newsroom.cisco.com/c/r/newsroom/en/us/a/y2020/m03/cisco-ranks-as-one-of-the-world-s-best-places-to-work-here-s-why.html.

79. Chan, "Cisco Ranks as One of the Best Places to Work."

80. *Inc.*, "Corporate Culture," Inc.com, accessed May 25, 2022, https://www.inc.com/encyclopedia/corporate-culture.html.

81. Richard Thompson Ford, "A Brief History of Dress Codes in the Workplace," *Fortune*, accessed July 16, 2022, https://fortune.com/longform/office-dress-codes-casual-friday-history-book-excerpt-richard-thompson-ford/.

82. Elka Torpey, "Women Managers," Bureau of Labor Statistics, accessed July 16, 2022, https://www.bls.gov/careeroutlook/2017/data-on-display/women-managers.htm#:~:text=In%202016%2C%20nearly%2040%20percent,half%20of%20workers%20were%20women.

83. Te-ping Chen, "Why Are There Still So Few Black CEOs?," *Wall Street Journal*, accessed July 1, 2022, https://www.wsj.com/articles/why-are-there-still-so-few-black-ceos-11601302601.

84. Amanda Reed, "A Brief History of Sexual Harassment in the United States," NOW.org, accessed April 16, 2022, https://now.org/blog/a-brief-history-of-sexual-harassment-in-the-united-states/#:~:text=Cornell%20University%20activists%20coined%20the,issue%20has%20risen%20since%20then.

85. Roger D. Duncan, "Culture, Leadership, Performance: How Are They Linked?," *Forbes*, accessed May 16, 2022, https://www.forbes.com/sites/rodgerdeanduncan/2018/10/30/culture-leadership-performance-how-are-they-linked/?sh=1530ba135e44.

86. Jeanne Meister, "The Future of Work Is Worker Well-Being," *Forbes*, accessed June 28, 2022, https://www.forbes.com/sites/jeannemeister/2021/08/04/the-future-of-work-is-worker-well-being/?sh=12af24514aed.

87. Meister, "The Future of Work Is Worker Well-Being."

88. Jennifer Liu, "Gallop: U.S. Are Among the Most Stressed in the World," CNBC.com, accessed July 16, 2022, https://www.cnbc.com/2021/06/15/gallup-us-workers-are-among-the-most-stressed-in-the-world.html.

89. Helen Tobler, "Eight Things Employees Expect in the Workplace in 2022," Seek.com, accessed July 1, 2022, https://www.seek.com.au/employer/hiring-advice/9-things-employees-expect-in-a-workplace-in-2021.

90. Andrew Martins, "International Survey Suggests Workers Care More for Company Culture Than Salary" Business News Daily, accessed July 1, 2022, https://www.businessnewsdaily.com/15206-company-culture-matters-to-workers.html.

91. Elizabeth A. Harris, "HarperCollins Union Workers strike for Increased Wages, Benefits, and Diversity," *New York Times*, July 20, 2022, https://www.nytimes.com/2022/07/20/books/harpercollins-strike.html?campaign_id=9&emc=edit_nn_20220723&instance_id=67460&nl=the-morning&regi_id=102361496&segment_

id=99383&te=1&user_id=a789f62565896555378ad
12c36770994.

92.   Lindsay Kolowich Cox, "27 Mission and Value Statements That Will
      Inspire Your Buyers," HubSpot, accessed July 1, 2022, https://blog.
      hubspot.com/marketing/inspiring-company-mission-statements.

93.   Cox, "27 Mission and Value Statements."

94.   Cox, "27 Mission and Value Statements."

95.   Your Dictionary, "Best Examples of Strong Company Vision State-
      ments," Your Dictionary, accessed June 29, 2022, https://examples.
      yourdictionary.com/best-examples-of-a-vision-statement.html.

96.   Your Dictionary, "Best Examples of Strong Company Vision
      Statements."

97.   Ikea.com, accessed August 22, 2022.

98.   Cox, "27 Mission and Value Statements."

99.   Yvon Chouinard, "Yvon Chouinard Donates Patagonia to Fight
      Climate Crisis," patagonia.com (Patagonia, Inc., 2022), https://www.
      patagonia.com/ownership/.

100. Sans Mirror, "Sony Kando 2.0," Sans Mirror, accessed July
      18, 2022, https://www.sansmirror.com/newsviews/2018-mir-
      rorless-camera-2/april-june-2018-newsviews/sony-kando-20.
      html#:~:text=Indeed%2C%20then%20Sony%20CEO%20
      Kazuo,by%20a%20spirit%20of%20kando.%E2%80%9D.

101. Sony Pictures, "Who We Are," Sony Pictures, accessed August 1,
      2022, https://www.sonypicturesjobs.com/who-we-are.

102. Kathryn Moody, "Marriott Shares Its 'Secret Sauce' for a People-
      Centric Culture," HRDive.com, accessed June 20, 2022, https://

www.hrdive.com/news/marriott-shares-its-secret-sauce-for-a-people-centric-culture/551369/.

103. Moody, "Marriott Shares Its 'Secret Sauce.'"

104. Moody, "Marriott Shares Its 'Secret Sauce.'"

105. Moody, "Marriott Shares Its 'Secret Sauce.'"

106. Starbucks, "Starbucks College Achievement Plan," Starbucks.com, accessed July 18, 2022, https://www.starbucksbenefits.com/en-us/home/education-opportunity/starbucks-college-achievement-plan/.

107. Kayleigh Bateman, "Company Culture Is Key to Keeping the Best People: Here's What Employees Value Most," World Economic Forum, accessed July 1, 2022, https://www.weforum.org/agenda/2021/11/good-company-culture-employee-great-resignation/#:~:text=Employees%20cite%20feeling%20respected%20as,ways%20to%20improve%20company%20culture.

108. Bateman, "Company Culture Is Key to Keeping the Best People."

109. David Burkus, "How Does Leadership Influence Organizational Culture?," DavidBurkus.com, accessed July 16, 2022, https://davidburkus.com/2022/04/how-does-leadership-influence-organizational-culture/.

110. Burkus, "How Does Leadership Influence Organizational Culture?"

111. Burkus, "How Does Leadership Influence Organizational Culture?"

112. Glen Stansberry, "10 Examples of Tremendous Business Leadership," AmericanExpress.com, accessed June 28, 2022, https://www.americanexpress.com/en-us/business/trends-and-insights/articles/10-examples-of-tremendous-business-leadership-1/.

113. Stansberry, "10 Examples of Tremendous Business Leadership."

114. Irene Jiang, "Costco Founder Warned CEO Not to Raise the Hot Dog Price," *Business Insider*, September 21, 2020, https://www.businessinsider.com/costco-founder-warned-ceo-not-to-raise-hot-dog-price-2020-9.

115. *Merriam-Webster*, "Integrity," Merriam-Webster.com, accessed July 14, 2022, https://www.merriam-webster.com/dictionary/integrity.

116. Purdue University Global, "How Does Workplace Diversity Actually Affect Business?" PurdueGlobal.edu, accessed June 14, 2022, https://www.purdueglobal.edu/blog/careers/how-does-workplace-diversity-affect-business/#:~:text=Diversity%20Improves%20Employee%20Retention%20and,company%20fosters%20an%20inclusive%20culture.

117. Purdue University Global, "How Does Workplace Diversity Actually Affect Business?"

118. Purdue University Global, "How Does Workplace Diversity Actually Affect Business?"

119. Reliable Plant, "Workplace Bad Apples Spoil Barrels of Good Employees," ReliablePlant.com, accessed July 20, 2022, https://www.reliableplant.com/Read/4768/workplace-bad-apples.

120. Scott Tuning, "Religious Inclusion in the Workplace: Definition, Benefits & Examples," Study.com (Study), accessed November 29, 2022, https://study.com/academy/lesson/religious-inclusion-in-the-workplace-definition-benefits-examples.html.

121. Diversity Abroad, "Japan," DiversityAbroad.com, accessed July 13, 2022, https://www.diversityabroad.com/articles/travel-guide/japan.

122. Wikipedia, "Fraunhofer Society," Wikipedia.org, accessed July 18, 2022, https://en.wikipedia.org/wiki/Fraunhofer_Society.

123. "MCSE (Microsoft Certified Systems Engineer) Salary," https://www.erieri.com/ (Economic Research Institute), accessed November 29, 2022, https://www.erieri.com/salary/job/mcse-microsoft-certified-systems-engineer/united-states.

Chiradeep BasuMallick, "CCNA Certification: Exam Cost, Salary, and Jobs in 2022," spiceworks.com, July 25, 2022, https://www.spiceworks.com/tech/networking/articles/what-is-ccna-certification/#:~:text=Applications%20in%202022-,CCNA%20Salary,as%20of%20June%208%2C%202022.

"CPA Salary and Career Guide," https://www.efficientlearning.com/,, Wiley Efficient Learning, accessed November 29, 2022, https://www.efficientlearning.com/cpa/resources/cpa-salary-breakdown/.

124. Ela Chodyniescka et al., "Money Can't Buy Your Employees' Loyalty," March 28, 2022.

125. Tradesman International, "Addressing a Welder Shortage in the Construction Industry," TradesmenInternational.com, accessed August 22, 2022, https://www.tradesmeninternational.com/construction-management/welder-shortage/.

126. Softstart, "4 Companies Who Nailed the New Employee Onboarding Experience," Softstart.com, May 19, 2022, https://softstart.app/blog/best-employee-onboarding-examples/.

127. Softstart, "4 Companies Who Nailed the New Employee Onboarding Experience."

128. Softstart, "4 Companies Who Nailed the New Employee Onboarding Experience."

129. Investopedia.com, "Which Countries are Most Important in Electronics?" accessed July 24, 2022, https://www.investopedia.com/ask/answers/042915/what-countries-contribute-largest-weight-global-electronics-sector.asp.

130. Wikipedia, "Jabil," Wikipedia.org, accessed July 25, 2022, https://en.wikipedia.org/wiki/Jabil#cite_note-7.

131. Global Opportunity Initiative, "5 Companies That Are Investing in Upskilling the Workforce," GOI, accessed July 23, 2022, https://goi.mit.edu/2022/04/21/five-companies-investing-in-upskilling-the-workforce/.

132. Global Opportunity Initiative, "5 Companies That Are Investing in Upskilling the Workforce."

133. Global Opportunity Initiative, "5 Companies That Are Investing in Upskilling the Workforce."

134. Global Opportunity Initiative, "5 Companies That Are Investing in Upskilling the Workforce."

135. Global Opportunity Initiative, "5 Companies That Are Investing in Upskilling the Workforce."

136. Maria Flynn, "Google.org Supports JFF's Outcomes for Opportunity Initiative with $4 Million Grant," jff.org (Jobs for the Future (JFF), 2020), https://www.jff.org/what-we-do/impact-stories/awake/outcomes-opportunity/googleorg-supports-jff/.

137. Global Opportunity Initiative, "5 Companies That Are Investing in Upskilling the Workforce."

138. Dorie Clark, "Google's 20 Percent Rule Shows Exactly How Much Time You Should Spend Learning New Skills—and Why It Works," CNBC.com, accessed July 25, 2022, https://www.cnbc.com/2021/12/16/google-20-percent-rule-shows-exactly-how-much-time-you-should-spend-learning-new-skills.html#:~:text=Enter%3A%20Google's%20%E2%80%9C20%25%20time,wrote%20in%20their%20IPO%20letter.

139. Clark, "Google's 20 Percent Rule."

140. Michael Lipka and Claire Gecewicz, "More Americans Now Say They're Spiritual but Not Religious," Pew Research Center, accessed July 24, 2022, https://www.pewresearch.org/fact-tank/2017/09/06/more-americans-now-say-theyre-spiritual-but-not-religious/#:~:text=About%20a%20quarter%20of%20U.S.,June%20 4%20of%20this%20year.

141. Religious Freedom & Business Foundation, "Socioeconomic Impact of Religious Freedom," Religious Freedom & Business Foundation, accessed July 23, 2022, https://religiousfreedomandbusiness.org/ socioeconomic-impact-of-religious-freedom.

142. Religious Freedom & Business Foundation, "Socioeconomic Impact of Religious Freedom."

143. PwC, "Millennials at Work," PwC.com, accessed October 12, 2022.

144. Amy Adkins and Brandon Rigoni, "Millennials Want Jobs to Be Development Opportunities," Gallup.com, accessed October 12, 2022.

145. Bureau of Labor Statistics, "Job Openings and Labor Turnover Summary: 2022 M08 Results," bls.gov, accessed October 11, 2022.

146. Kim Parker and Juliana Menasce Horowitz, "The Great Resignation: Why Workers Say They Quit Jobs in 2021," Pew Research Center, March 9, 2022.

147. Andrew Chamberlain, "Why Do Employees Stay? A Clear Career Path and Good Pay, for Starters," *Harvard Business Review*, March 6, 2017.

148. Center for American Progress, "There Are Significant Business Costs to Replacing Employees," Center for American Progress, accessed October 12, 2022.

149. Anderson Pinheiro Cavalcanti, "Automatic Feedback in Online Learning Environments: A Systematic Literature Review," accessed October 12, 2022, https://doi.org/10.1016/j.caeai.2021.100027.

150. "Generation Differences Chart," usf.edu (University of South Florida), accessed November 29, 2022, https://www.usf.edu/hr-training/documents/lunch-bytes/generationaldifferenceschart.pdf.